J**US**TICE
BY DESIGN

GUIDE TO CREATING

CURRICULUM FOR SOCIAL JUSTICE

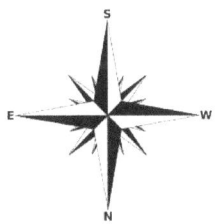

IAN B. MCLAUGHLIN

Copyright © 2021 Ian B. McLaughlin

All rights reserved.

Paperback: 978-1-7366061-0-0

Audiobook: 978-1-7366061-2-4

Ebook: 978-1-7366061-1-7

First paperback edition March 2021.

Copyedited by Darya C. at Ebook Launch
Cover art by Ian B. McLaughlin
Photography by Danny Smith
Layout by Justice By Design LLC

Justice by Desgin LLC
Minneapolis, MN

www.JusticeByDesign.org

Table of Contents

Introduction

Part I: The Why

1. My Personal, Local, and Immediate Why
2. Context: A Two-Track System
3. Building Intention: Purpose and Vision for Curriculum Oriented Toward Social Justice
4. Believing: Love Is Justice

Part II: The How

5. Do Your Self-Work
6. Nurture Interdependence
7. Stay Grounded

Part III: The What

8. Phase Theory
9. Rigor and Standards
10. Pedagogies Oriented Toward Social Justice
11. Backward Planning and Social Justice
12. Understanding for Social Justice
13. Assessment for Social Justice
14. Putting It All Together
15. Reflect and Restore

Introduction

Let me begin with gratitude. Thank you for opening up *Justice by Design*. Really. Thank you for giving your time and energy to this book. As a person with a reading disability, who did not learn how to read until later in life, I know firsthand the kind of time and energy it can take to open, process, and work through a book.

You should know right off that I have many beliefs, many of which will be apparent throughout the following pages, but a few I will just come out and tell you. I believe in the power of gratitude.

When my first daughter was born, I had crippling anxiety for her safety. I had images of falling down the stairs with her in my arms every morning. I had images of her stroller getting hit by a car or bicycle every time I crossed the street with her. I had images of her choking on literally everything each time she coughed or reached for an object. I could not sleep for fear of her not breathing in her sleep. I could not function due to the constant fear I felt in my stomach and chest. I could not exist without a flash of the most horrible vivid depictions of the unthinkable every couple of minutes.

Finally, I found my medicine for this crippling anxiety in mindful gratitude. Every time a flash of the worst passed into my body, I looked at my daughter and concentrated on how thankful

INTRODUCTION

I was she was healthy and safe and loved. Gratitude pushed the fear out of my body until the next minute when a new fear squeezed between my stomach and lungs. However, eventually, the worry lessened with each moment of gratitude to the point where I could function again.

I was very thankful for this.

As I am thankful for the multitude of teachers and students in my life who helped to shape my beliefs and helped me grow in my practice as an educator, I am also still thankful you have made it this far into *Justice by Design*.

...

Again, I have many beliefs. Like strong instruction stems from strong questions and leads toward deep, enduring understanding and that storytelling is essential to deep, enduring understanding. I also believe this book models strong instruction in many ways:

- ❖ What brought you to open *Justice by Design*?
- ❖ What do you hope to gain from giving this book your time and energy?
- ❖ What has social justice meant in your personal story?
- ❖ What does it mean to be an educator, a teacher, a student, a parent, or a curriculum writer in our current collective story?

...

This book exists in the context of our current realities. We have a system of "Injustice by Design" in the US that continually gets the results that were intended, a system that I have personally benefited from my entire life due to unearned advantages from my privileged identity markers as a cisgender White man from a socioeconomically stable family growing up in New York City. I believe it is important to begin by naming my privileged identity markers and by naming that *despite* being in education my entire life—as a student with disabilities, a teacher with "good intentions," a school administrator, educational coach, and teacher of teachers—I need to be a consummate learner. In fact, cross out "despite" in the previous sentence, and write "because." *Because* I've been in education my entire life, I need to be a consummate learner and, oftentimes, an unlearner, to move from "Injustice by Design" toward *Justice*.

Justice by Design does not shy away from naming the positions we hold in society. Instead, it is precisely due to these positions, and the privileges that come with them, that require someone with my identity markers to work toward deconstructing oppressive systems which, literally in far too many cases, cost people who have been oppressed all their lives but also come at a steep price for those of us occupying positions of privilege.

Justice by Design means to intentionally design curriculum oriented toward social justice. At its root, *Justice by Design* is really

INTRODUCTION

an analysis of intentions. Given that, this book has a very specific intention.

This book exists to support educators in using the tenants of backward planning to intentionally create rigorous interdisciplinary curriculum oriented toward social justice and to repair harm that may be caused along the way.

To accomplish this intention, this book intertwines (1) personal narratives with (2) teachings from visionaries working toward social justice with (3) concrete tools for educators to implement. Along this road, I have sought to merge work by bell hooks, Bettina Love, Adrienne Maree Brown, Lisa Delpit, Paulo Freire, Peggy McIntosh, Jondou Chase Chen, Sharon Salzberg, and Parker Palmer to name a few with the principals of *Understanding by Design* by McTighe and Wiggins and Simon Sinek's Golden Circle. I believe the power in this book lies in taking the principles of *Understanding by Design* and Sinek's Golden Circle and clearly steering them toward social justice.

I believe another power in this book lies in the personal narratives you will find throughout its pages. You should know now that I love telling stories, and every chapter contains at least one.

You should also know that I love organization.

This book was written with several clearly organized guiding structures. One of these organizational structures has been to highlight the many significant identities of the voices shared in this text in an effort to both honor the intersecting identities of individuals quoted and provide more context for their words that matters at this point in time. To this end, I have attempted to include self-described identities such as race, ethnicity, gender, sexual orientation, and occupation among others—gleaned from artist statements, writings, and in some cases personal correspondence.

Another organizing structure was to divide the book into three parts: (I) The Why, (II) The How, and (III) The What. Part I begins by building intentions toward social justice, Part II moves on to name-guiding values that grow from our intentions, and Part III provides tools for educators to enact their intentions, as well as reflect and repair from our practice. Each chapter is also broken into five identical segments (you might start to notice my compulsions with organization at this point):

1. Opening Quotation: to hook you right away, illuminate the connectedness of this work, and generally demonstrate that what this book is saying has been said before...though I still highly recommend you read it.
2. Question(s): in the form of either deep essential questions or more focused guiding questions—modeling that the strongest instruction stems from strong questions.
3. The Narrative: personal stories from my own experiences as an educator, a student, and a human.

4. The Body: covers the rationale and/or significance behind the chapter's key content and often includes tools teachers can use, along with a synthesis of research findings and/or words from people working toward social justice.
5. The Recap and Moving Forward: provides a summary of sorts and a preview of what's to come next. If you are trying to read this book in a matter of minutes and are not a speed reader, this might be a place to focus.

Given the structures present, how should one actually read *Justice by Design*?

How one reads a book has always been an important question for someone like myself who struggled immensely to learn to read growing up. Today, this question is always front and center when I pick up a book because since I learned to read (albeit much later in my life than many), I have rarely been one to read a book cover to cover unless it starts with the words Harry and Potter.

So, there are many ways to read this book for a variety of learners. If you learn through storytelling, focus on "The Narrative" for each chapter. If you learn by doing, focus on part III of this book (i.e., chapters 8–13). If you are averse to linearity, read the chapters in whatever order you like; they may point you in spiraling patterns anyway. If you build belief by reviewing reasoning and research, skip to the body of each chapter. If you are a type A detail-oriented learner, then read every line of each chapter and make sure to take notes in the margin. If you are an auditory learner, listen to the audio or read it out loud to your cats each night. If you are just not that into reading, get two copies, give one to a friend, ask them to summarize the book for you, and then put your copy on the shelf, point to it when anyone walks into the room, and extoll on how it clearly changed your life. If you're a kinesthetic learner, come up with an interpretive dance after each chapter and share them on YouTube—I'd love to see them. The point being, there are many ways to enjoy and utilize *Justice by Design*. I only hope that you do *utilize* this resource, *rewrite* your curriculums, *redesign* your classrooms, and *reimagine* education to support scholars in becoming change makers—changing the narrative of our collective story.

Part I

The Why

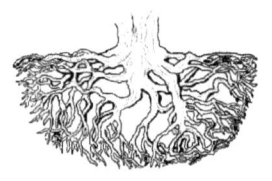

Chapter 1

My Personal, Local, and Immediate Why

For most people, medicine is something used to treat or cure a disease, often a man-made drug or sometimes an herb. Sometimes it refers to the whole field of medicine: hospitals, pharmacies, doctors, and so on. In Native traditions, however, medicine is a way of achieving balance. An Indigenous medicine person doesn't just heal illnesses—he or she can restore harmony or establish a state of being, like peacefulness. Medicine people live and practice among the people; access to them is constant and unrestricted. And the practice of medicine is not just limited to the hands of medicine people: everyone is welcome to participate. Engaging with medicine is a part of the experience of daily life. Traditionally, Indigenous people don't wait to be out of balance before they turn to medicine.

— EDGAR VILLANUEVA (2018), SELF IDENTIFIES AS A LUMBEE MAN.

Essential Question: Why is this work personally important?

Narrative: My First Year Teaching

In my first year of teaching, I had the privilege of working with Kayci as her Special Education case manager. She was in the 12th grade when I met her. She had a traumatic brain injury from asphyxiation at birth, and her file stated that most likely as a result of the brain injury she scored in the developmental disability range on tests of cognitive ability (in older terminology, this would have been defined as Mental Retardation). Her mom, a single mother who struggled with substance abuse, was a fierce advocate for Kayci. When I asked Kayci about her father, she generally noted he was an asshole and often left it there. She identified as a biracial Black and White woman. She had dreams. She wanted to be a veterinarian. I mean, both she and her mother asserted how her entire life her dream was to become a veterinarian for small animals. She took the two advanced placement classes our school had to offer seniors: Statistics and Anatomy and Physiology. In general, she was a very hardworking and focused student.

One day she came into my office crying after having spoken with a county counselor. The counselor had told her to give up her dream. The counselor did not know her. She looked at Kayci's paperwork and said someone with her disability could not become a veterinarian. The counselor said her best option for postsecondary education was a trade school of some sort—probably cosmetology (note: I am not disparaging cosmetology here or trade schools, but Kayci had no interest in these).

Kayci was broken up after this meeting, and so she came to me. We had only known each other for half a year at this point, but there was trust between us. Kayci mattered to me, and I believe she felt this. She didn't ask for anything when she came to me. She just needed space to share her grief.

Over ten years later, I can still remember the moment. I remember it because I thought her story was my story. I was told by the teacher I trusted most in 12th grade, Mr. Sternstein, "College isn't for everyone, Ian," despite my dreams to complete college. I knew at the time my teacher's words had come from a place of love because of my personal challenges as a person with learning disabilities in school, but I also knew that he was wrong. College was for me, despite my learning disabilities—dyslexia and ADHD. I went on to graduate from Landmark College, a two-year program for students with disabilities, motivated to prove my former teacher wrong. I went on to earn my bachelor's degree as the only person in my department to graduate with honors that year and as a published author. I then graduated from my master's program with a 4.0. Now I both teach graduate-level courses and coach adjunct professors teaching preservice teachers. I know from personal experience that Mr. Sternstein was wrong about me. And I thought Kayci's story was my story.

We both had dreams. We both had disabilities. We were both told in so many words that because of our disabilities we could not achieve our dreams.

I told Kayci, "Forget what the counselor told you! She is wrong! You can achieve any dreams you want. But know that when you have a disability, it means that you are going to have to work three to five times as hard just to scrape by. It means you are going to need to join every study group and spend every spare minute in the library to get by with Cs, but if you keep up that mentality, the Cs will become Bs, which will become As—and I am proof that you can do this. Because this is my story." I told her about my high school teacher's words and my educational path.

Kayci was reinvigorated. She already worked hard in school, but she worked harder. Her mom who I often spoke with thanked me time and again for believing in Kayci and sharing my story with her. She said the counselor's words had broken Kayci down, but my words brought her back.

Kayci got into a small private liberal arts college that had fantastic support for students with disabilities as well as for first-generation college students, which Kayci was. I thought with that program and Kayci's drive, she could make it. She could reach her goal of becoming a veterinarian. Because her story is my story...

Kayci never made it to that small liberal arts college though; they did not offer enough financial aid. In addition to her financial aid package, she needed to find just over $8,000 more dollars to start the program. Instead, Kayci went to the local community college where she could attend for free and work part time. Eventually, over a decade later, Kayci did not reach her dreams.

Kayci's story was very different from mine. Hers lacked the privilege I was taught to be oblivious to in my story. My family could afford to send me to two private colleges for five years to obtain my bachelor's degree. Prior to that, I went to a private high school in New York City, which had a high level of rigor—my Cs there represented much more rigorous work than As at the public school where I taught Kayci. I am also a cisgender White man, so the doors kept opening for me regardless of how many spelling errors or past failures I had. The privileges I was granted as a White man with disabilities from a socioeconomically stable family in New York City are not universal.

Kayci's story was *not* my story.

Why *Justice by Design*?

Because I wish I was more intentional about supporting Kayci to reach her goals. I believe Kayci's counselor was wrong to crush her dreams and that I was right to reinforce them with words, but I failed to reinforce her dreams with understanding and action. I wish I would have talked to Kayci's councilor. I wish I would not have taken Kayci's mother's misplaced trust in me for granted and instead been much more critical of myself. I wish I would have told Kayci that working hard on assignments well below grade-level rigor will not prepare you for your dreams—we are setting you up for failure here. I wish I could have told her, "I'm sorry. Let's change that. Let's work on going above and beyond, because you can go above and beyond what we are working on here, and you need to if you are going to achieve your dreams." *Justice by Design* demands high expectations.

I wish I had understood what high expectations were and that we need to do more than have high expectations; we need to tell the truth. I wish I had understood more about the truth of intersecting systems of oppression. *Justice by Design* requires honesty, authenticity in tune with our realities, and an intersectional[1] analysis of the world to harness the transformative power of education.

Why *Justice by Design*? Because I can't go back and repair the harm I caused Kayci—Kayci and countless other students. I can't go back and repair the hurt caused by reinforcing the myths of meritocracy, the soft bigotry of low expectations[2] and false narratives rampant in our society. I can't go back, but I can support future educators in not making my mistakes. *Justice by Design* is meant to interrupt educators in making the mistakes I made and continue to make and, instead, build opportunities for hope.

Throughout the narratives in this book, you will read a plethora of my failures from my first teaching jobs to my latest endeavors. I constantly work to reimagine my perceived failures as opportunities for growth. *Justice by Design* was born as much from my successes as from my failures. So, this book was not written from the perspective of a master educator with all the answers. I am not, and *the* answer will not be found in these pages. What is located in these pages is authentic and strives to open the doors to both personal growth and social justice.

---

[1] See pages 75–78 for a description of *intersectionality*.
[2] The idea of teaching less, down, or for remediation is often referred to as "the soft bigotry of low expectations" (Bush, 2006).

Why *Justice by Design*? Because I have two Latina daughters, and I want their teachers to be better than me. I want them to have access to all the opportunities I deprived my female students of color, like Kayci, because I lacked the tools, personal reflection, and beliefs inherent in understanding how to develop a curriculum oriented toward social justice. Because I was oblivious to my ignorance. Because I did not know what I did not know as the system intended.

Why *Justice by Design*? Because it is the responsibility of White people like myself to work toward disrupting and dismantling White supremacy. It is the responsibility of men like myself to disrupt and deconstruct patriarchy. And it is the responsibility of the beneficiaries of capitalism like myself to disrupt and demolish exploitative capitalism. *Justice by Design* strives to tear down the intersectional White supremacist capitalist patriarchy[3].

Why *Justice by Design*? Because it is part of my personal healing from the disease of colonization. Make no mistake, while colonization literally brought about the genocide of native people in the Americas, and ultimately led to the mass incarceration of Black and Brown people today, it is also a disease for us White folks, a disease that eats away at my personal humanity. My loss deepens every time I view those who are different as *others*, every

---

[3] A reference to bell hook's term; see page 85 for a brief description.

time I treat those who are different as *others*, every time I fear *the other*, all disconnecting me from my brothers and sisters, from my ancestry, and from my own body. Writing *Justice by Design* has been medicine to me. Writing curricula using the tenets of *Justice by Design* is medicine to me. It requires me to think, act, believe, feel, and reconnect—writing this centers me and breathes balance into my being.

Justice by Design is meant to support healing.

Recap and Moving Forward

Justice by Design is guided by the goal to support educators in using the tenants of backward planning to intentionally create rigorous interdisciplinary curriculum oriented toward social justice and to repair harm that may be caused along the way. *Justice by Design* is about social justice, high expectations, authenticity, and more. It is about personal healing. It is about finding your personal meaning, wholeness[4], and center[5] in education as much as it is about social change. "For most people, medicine is something used to treat or cure a disease, often a man-made drug or sometimes an herb... In Native traditions, however, medicine is a way of achieving balance... And the practice of medicine is not just

---

[4] A reference to Peggy McIntosh's Phase Theory; see chapter 8 for an in-depth discussion.

[5] A reference to Courageous Conversations; see page 222-223 for a brief summary.

limited to the hands of medicine people: everyone is welcome to participate." (Villanueva, 2018)

We have not arrived. We have not arrived as a nation. We have not arrived as an educational system. I have not personally arrived as a cisgender White male educator. But I am working on it, working toward wholeness and center. *Justice by Design* represents my personal work as much as it represents one of many paths for orienting classrooms toward social justice.

Chapter 2

Context: A Two-Track System

Every system is perfectly designed to get the results it gets.

— ATTRIBUTED TO MULTIPLE AUTHORS (CONWAY & BATALDEN, 2015)

Guiding Question: How would you define each track discussed in this chapter?

Narrative: My Family History

My great-great-grandmother was the child of Irish and English immigrants who came to North America, California specifically, in 1855. They called my great-great-grandmother the, "The Boss." My aunt, who shared this history with me, notes how The Boss's name conjures mixed emotions, both pride and endearment, believing her name exemplified her ability to get things done as a strong, assertive single mother, along with feelings of unease, noting that were she a man they probably would not have called her The Boss for such dispositions. The Boss did get things done and dramatically changed our family's trajectory.

Irish folk coming to California at that time period were often coming from Australia, not Ireland. Why were Irish folk in Australia? They were most likely shipped there as convicts due to any number of high offenses such as speaking out for labor rights or an inability to pay taxes. In other words, if you were poor or pro-labor, there was a good chance you were breaking the law and had to either leave to colonize native Aboriginal people's land in Australia or spend your time in work camps back in the homeland. My family actually has no idea why our ancestors came to the US by way of Australia. Whenever my grandfather asked his grandmother, The Boss, she snapped at him, "That's none of your damn business, young man!" And that was that.

The Boss eventually married another Irishman, William McLaughlin, who died by age forty, most likely due to alcoholism and drug abuse, but again, whenever my grandfather asked The Boss about her late husband, the response was always the same, "That's none of your damn business, young man." And that was that.

The Boss was fortunate to work as the personal secretary for William Randolph Hearst's wife, Phoebe. William Randolph Hearst was a wealthy industrialist known for developing the nation's largest newspaper chain and media company at the time. The Boss and her only son, my great-grandfather, lived on the Hearst estate in San Simeon for a time while The Boss worked for Phoebe. Back in the early 1900s, this kind of job was a privilege many other descendants of ex-cons from non-White-presenting racial groups probably wouldn't have access to, and it did bring numerous privileges. One of the most important privileges was access to a quality education for The Boss's son, my great-grandfather. William Randolph Hearst paid for my great-grandfather, known to us as "Viejo,"[6] to go to grade school, and then college, and then set him up with connections for a career in education after college. Viejo went on to become a geology professor at Harvard University and ultimately a chairman of the Board of Regents of the University of California, where there is a building named after him in his honor.

I never met Viejo; he passed away two years before I was born, but he did have two sons with his first wife: Charlie and Donald. Charlie went on to become the foremost historian on the landscape architect Frederick Law Olmsted and a professor at the American University in DC. Donald dropped out of high school to join the navy at age seventeen, forging his draft documents. However, after World War II, Donald went back to school, finished his high school diploma, and then received two advanced degrees in geology. He decided to drop out of college again one semester shy of completing his PhD to work for California Standard Oil (now Chevron) as a geologist.

Donald was my grandfather, Grandpa Don. Growing up, Grandpa Don always told me to go to college and not to drop out before I finished my degrees like he did...twice. He knew how important college was and the doors it opened.

---

[6] While the grandchildren of Irish and English immigrants, my father's generation grew up in South America speaking both English and Spanish.

One could argue that both The Boss and Viejo set my entire family on a track toward college that would proliferate for generations: seven out of seven of Viejo's great-grandchildren past college age hold bachelor's degrees, and five out of seven of us hold advanced post-baccalaureate degrees. Despite the fact that Viejo's grandparents were most likely ex-convicts without any formal schooling, despite the fact that Viejo came from a group of people who were oppressed at the time (in the early 1900s Irish were not considered White and were therefore excluded from many White privileges now afforded the ancestors of Irish immigrants), and despite having a father struggling with substance abuse and dying young, *education* leveled the playing field for Viejo. In my family's history, education has been the great equalizer.

This is the narrative I grew up with, a narrative I saw reinforced by the media, politicians, and society at large in the US for much of my life. But as with many narratives I grew up with, it is a myth served to support the dominant group.

Viejo would not have beaten the odds without the support of a wealthy industrialist who benefited from the exploitation of countless Irish immigrants among others during the Gilded Age. Viejo was the exception that proves the rule is real. Was Viejo hard working and smart and almost as good looking as his great-grandson, Ian? Sure, at least that's what I've been told. But what made the key difference was the support of a wealthy industrialist. If there were actual equal access to quality education at the time regardless of race or class or sex, there would be no need for exceptions, no need for beating the odds. But there was not equal access to quality education when Viejo went to school, and there has not been since.

A Two-Track System

Thomas Jefferson, author of the Declaration of Independence, former president, owner of enslaved peoples, and rapist, was also largely praised as one of the most adamant supporters of public education among our country's founders by other famous, and also dead, old White guys like John Dewey. During his life, Jefferson proposed a two-track school system, which would separate workers from the "learned" class. This was clearly noted in a letter Jefferson wrote to Peter Carr in 1814:

> *Every citizen... should receive an education proportioned to the condition and pursuits of his life. the mass of our citizens may be divided into two classes, the laboring, & the learned. the laboring will need the first grade of education to qualify them for their pursuits and duties: the learned will need it as a foundation for further acquirements... At the discharge of the pupils from this elementary school, the two classes separate... The learned class may still be subdivided into two sections. 1. those who are destined for learned professions as a means of livelihood; and 2. the Wealthy who possessing independent fortunes may aspire to share in conducting the affairs of the nation, or to live with usefulness & respect in the private ranks of life. Both of these sections will require instruction in all the higher branches of science, the wealthy to qualify them for either public or private life, the Professional section will need those*

branches especially which are the basis of their future profession. (Jefferson, 1814)

Sound familiar? Let's read one key sentence again: "The mass of our citizens may be divided into two classes, the laboring and the learned." Jefferson is proposing a two-track public education system.

Contrary to what many believe, the Constitution of the United States does not explicitly guarantee the right to a quality education. Challenges to the quality of education have had to utilize the equal protection clause of the 14th Amendment to work toward educational equity.

As a result, Jefferson's two tracks are largely in place three hundred years later. Moving beyond binaries,[7] I should note that when I say "two tracks," I recognize that there is a gray area between them—a continuum that may appear more as a bimodal distribution. Beyond the gray, in the aggregate, in the US today, there are real and disparate outcomes whether you make it onto the college track or not. Among people over age twenty-five, those with a bachelor's degree had median annual earnings of $64,896 in 2020, compared with $38,792 for those with only a high-school education (US Bureau of Labor Statistics, 2020). That equates to earning more than 1 million more dollars over the course of one's life with a college degree than without. It equates to "privileges" like increased opportunities for homeownership, the single biggest

---

[7] See pages 43 and 78-84 for a description of moving beyond binaries.

driver of generational wealth in our country's history. Today, the household income is one of, if not the greatest, correlate of student achievement according to numerous studies (Cahalan et al, 2018; Reardon, 2013). So ultimately, which track one ends up on perpetuates a generational vicious cycle because of the predictive educational outcomes associated with household incomes and educational levels.

Our educational system even pathologizes poverty, blaming people who are impoverished for these disparities and letting legislators, exploitative corporations, and educators—with our all-too-often low-rigor lesson plans—off the hook. Lisa Delpit (2012), an award-winning author and foremost educator and researcher on the subject of culturally relevant approaches to educating students of color and self-identified Black woman, writes in *Multiplication Is for White People*, "It is convenient to choose poverty as the reason for poor performance… blaming poverty works out for school systems because then you don't have to change your lesson plans!" However, due to the numerous exceptions that prove the rule, we also know that household income does not need to be deterministic—if given access to high-quality educational opportunities, any student regardless of socioeconomic status can enjoy the privileges offered by the "college track."

Seeing the deterministic nature of household income as a predictor of educational attainment in the aggregate is also not to say public education represents one track, and private education another. There are many private schools that perpetuate the noncollege track throughout this country, just as there are many high-achieving public-school districts and charter schools leading toward college. However, the majority of high-achieving public-school districts are united by a community of economically secure middle-class families with sufficient political power to demand great schools, the time and resources to participate in those schools, and the tax money to amply fund them. In general, perceived great public schools in terms of measures such as test scores, suspension rates, and family surveys are usually the product of a thriving middle class, not the other way around—as we come back to that whole gray area between our tracks.

Ultimately, the failure to truly educate all people has resulted in schools largely becoming sites of social reproduction. The wealthy and powerful send their children to schools with other wealthy and powerful children. They are taught the skills and norms necessary to maintain their status, power, and wealth. Meanwhile, the children of the working class and impoverished go to schools with other working class and impoverished families. They are taught a curriculum that represents the story of the wealthy and powerful. They enter buildings with police patrolling the hallways where educators have set the lowest expectations. When we really look at our system, it is clear that Jefferson's tracks are alive and profuse.

CONTEXT: A TWO-TRACK SYSTEM

It's hard to come to a conclusion other than that the purpose of schooling in the US is to maintain the social order, keeping power and resources in the hands of those who have traditionally hoarded both. Throughout our history, threats to this arrangement have been many: from the enslaved learning to read under the threat of death and The Black Panther Party's community schools to Ethnic Studies programs like the Mexican American Studies program in Arizona—communities that have been oppressed have always understood education as a pivotal part in the struggle to end oppression. Note, when I use the term *education* here, I am referring to the pursuit of learning and understanding, not *schooling* per se, which has so frequently been used as a tool of domination and assimilation (for an egregious example look to Native American boarding schools).

Those in power have time and again taken steps to leverage the power of the state, and its institutions, against upward mobility movements. Enslavers of Africans brutally punished or even killed the enslaved who pursued literacy; the Black Panthers were the main target of the FBI's COINTEL program; Arizona banned ethnic studies; and even *Brown v Board of Education* was co-opted and used as the basis to close highly successful all Black and all LatinX schools. *Brown v Board of Education* often lead to firing expert Black and Brown educators just to put Black and Brown students in buildings overseen by White folks who could maintain a racialized social order up close.

It's not often that public education is placed in this context. Public education is frequently discussed as the great equalizer, the key to combat oppression: from Horace Man (1848), creator of the common school movement, stating in the 1800's, "Education then, beyond all other devices of human origin, is a great equalizer of the conditions of men," to Arne Duncun restating in 2011 as the US Secretary of Education, "In America, education is still the great equalizer" (Brenchley, 2011). But we know this is not true by default. To make it true, we have to be intentional about facilitating the process.

Intention. Let's pause and focus on that word *intentional* for a moment.

Since the founding of the US, oppressive policies have been intentionally crafted, recrafted, and intentionally hidden to maintain the social order. Ibrim X. Kendi (2016), a foremost historian, leading antiracist voice, and self-identified Black man, details in *Stamped from the Beginning*, that contrary to popular dogma, racist policies (such as race-based chattel slavery, Jim Crow laws, or race-based "drug war" policies) do not arise from racist ideas pushed by ignorant hateful people. Rather, he breaks down how over three hundred years, time and again racist policies in the US led to racist ideas, which led to hate and ignorance. Let's look at the creation of Whiteness as an example of this intentional process at work.

The Creation of Whiteness

In the 1600s at the dawn of English colonization in North America, there were four primary groups of people present: Native Americans, wealthy English landholders, poor European peasants and indentured servants, and poor African peasants and slaves. There were differences between poor Africans and poor Europeans in the colonies during this early time period; for instance, Africans were brought to the colonies against their will (an understatement to say the least), while Europeans were often given a choice. However, once in the Americas, the similarities between these two groups were stronger than their differences. Both groups worked alongside each other in inhumane conditions, both groups could gain their freedom, and both groups could become members of the community after their enslavement/service period. Because both groups had far more in common with each other than either group had with English landholders or Native Americans, it was very common for intermarriage between African slaves and European indentured servants during this time. As the need for workers in the colonies grew, the working slave/servant class began to outnumber the English landholding class. Predicting a risky situation, English lawmakers attempted to separate these two groups by naming "negro and other slaves" or "negro, mulatto, and Indian slaves" and "Black slaves,"—trying to group and separate Africans as "black." However, merely naming African's as "negro," "mulatto," or "black" in law was not enough to separate them from their poor European brothers and sisters in bonds. (Battalora, 2013)

In 1676, the English landholder's fears were realized when African peasants and slaves banded with European peasants and indentured servants to rebel and burn down Jamestown Virginia—known as Bacon's Rebellion. This led English lawmakers in the colonies to write anti-miscegenation laws, which forbade intermarriage between racial groups. To accomplish this, it required lawmakers to create and solidify separate races—Black, White, and Native (at the time)—in efforts to forbid poor Africans from marrying poor Europeans. For example, Virginia law in 1691 stated, "Whatsoever English or other <u>white</u> man or woman being free shall intermarry with a negroe [sic], mulatto, or Indian man or woman bond or free, shall within three months after such marriage be banished and removed from the dominion forever." Prior to this, poor Europeans were named as "other Europeans," or "Christians." Here they are named as "<u>white</u>" for the first time. As such, Whiteness, and to a degree as well anti-Blackness[8], was born in the mind of America from legislative action. (Battalora, 2013)

This plan worked as it was intended. It ended all efforts of the majority of people in the colonies, African or Europeans, to fight for equal rights in the colonies against the powerful landowners who ruled everything. It reduced Africans to the status of permanent slave and gave the poor, but now *White* people, a precious and entitled inch to stand above the permanently enslaved on the social ladder. The next thing the politicians did sealed the deal: they paid poor Whites a bounty for runaway enslaved people and often made them overseers for enslaved people, turning every poor White person in the colonies into a prison guard against the people who had once been their neighbors, co-conspirators, and loved ones. They then reinforced anti-Black rhetoric and White supremacy rhetoric to support their racist and exploitative policies—dividing and conquering the working, indentured, and enslaved classes.

Jaqueline Battalora (2013), who self-identifies as female, White, sister, daughter, friend, queer, middle class, able bodied/mind, Catholic, parent, partner, teacher, speaker, and innovator writes in *Birth of a White Nation*, "The invention of white people has

---

[8] Anti-Blackness or anti-Black racism is often considered one of two pillars that uphold white supremacy in the US (in addition to the erasure of Native Americans). Anti-Blackness refers to a theoretical framework that illuminates society's inability to recognize humanity in Blackness. It includes institutions, policies, and rhetoric that strips Blackness of value (dehumanizes) and systematically marginalizes Black people.

> had a lasting impact not the least of which is the persistence of the belief that white people constitute a unique group of humanity—a race. The history of the invention of white people exposes the 'white race' for what it is: a historical creation to serve the interests of the wealthiest capitalists and provide unearned advantages for those labeled white, and unearned disadvantages to those labeled other-than-white. The invention has served the interests of the wealthiest by keeping laborers divided, viewing each other as competition along so-called race lines rather than collective strength... The invention of white people has worked not only to divide laborers from each other, but has caused white laborers to perceive a stronger link with those whose social condition and class is dramatically different from their own, on the sole basis of sharing a fictitious race." I encourage you to read *Birth of a White Nation* for an in-depth look into this process.

As noted in the preceding example, racist rhetoric was intentionally created to support exploitative policies. Policies drive racist ideology, not the other way around. Cycles like these have persisted for four hundred years because calculating men and women intentionally produce racist ideas to justify the racist policies of their era and redirect the blame for their era's racial and class disparities away from those policies; intentionally crafted racist ideas that have intertwined with the idea of a two-track education system produced not only class injustice but racial injustice as well.

We saw this pattern play out in the federal legislation titled No Child Left Behind (NCLB) in 2001. At its most basic level, NCLB stated it would hold schools and districts accountable for racial and socioeconomic disparities in standardized test scores by punishing schools and districts that failed to meet adequate yearly progress on tests of reading and math. While stating seemingly noble objectives, the law lacked acknowledgment or a means to address the fact that schools and districts across the country did not have equal or equitable access to resources and opportunities to meet the law's ambitious goals to start with. Meaning, the law was ultimately designed to punish schools and districts that were not set up to succeed in the first place. Not surprisingly, outcomes from the policy demonstrated continued racial and economic disparities. Ultimately, NCLB succeeded at redistributing more resources and support *away* from communities that have traditionally been denied resources and support for four hundred years. To justify policy outcomes like shifting resources away from struggling schools, the law ostensibly names Black youth in particular as deficient and needing to be fixed. The subtext of the legislation was if the law could not *fix* inadequate progress in math and reading in certain communities, then the problem must lie in the students from those communities, that is, *they* must be deficient, not the law.

Researcher and policy advocate Connie Wun (2014), who self identifies as an Asian woman writes, "[NCLB] Popularized and institutionalized national attention on Black youth as problems to be solved... Despite its beneficent claims to equalizing educational opportunities and outputs, the race-conscious mandate... is an instrument of Whiteness. The color-blind educational policy may claim intentions to redress racial inequalities, but its underpinnings and outcomes demonstrate otherwise. Contrary to the articulated claims of closing the achievement gap, NCLB naturalizes social inequalities. For instance, although schools do not receive adequate funding to meet NCLB mandates these students are blamed for failing to meet the standards because theoretically they were given ample opportunities to succeed. In addition, students who fail to meet the policy's racialized academic standards are stigmatized and further alienated."

Following this legislation, we witnessed another large shift in public P12 education in the US: an unprecedented increase in philanthropic dollars flooding into schools and policy reform via foundations like the Gates, Walton, and Broad. Lisa Delpit (2012) writes that public schools, "Have been overrun by the antidemocratic forces of extreme wealth. Educational policy for the past decade has largely been determined by the financial contributions of several very large corporate foundations. Among a few others, the Broad, Gates, and Walton (Walmart) foundations have dictated various 'reforms' by flooding the educational enterprise with capital. The ideas of privatization, charter schools, Teach for America, the extremes of the accountability movement, merit pay, increased standardized testing, free market competition—all are promulgated and financially supported by corporate foundations, which indeed have those funds because they can avoid paying the taxes that the rest of us must foot. Thus, educational policy has been virtually hijacked by the wealthiest citizens, whom no one elected and who are unlikely ever to have had a child in the public schools." Here we come back to intentionality; we come back to *why*; and back to purpose, vision, and beliefs.

I don't believe the intentions behind such philanthropic giving is innately evil—I think we need to move past such binaries. I question whether the intentions behind corporate foundations that benefit from managing extreme wealth and are federally incentivized to give money to avoid paying taxes could truly support public educational reforms oriented toward social justice, meaning reforms that strive for a just *redistribution* of wealth, opportunities, and resources. Or do such corporate foundations benefit too much from maintaining the status quo, albeit with some tweaking? Outcomes from the billions of private dollars pouring into public education over the past decade and a half continue to replicate the same outcomes we have seen on a large scale for hundreds of years, namely the outcome of a nuanced, but ever present, two-track educational system.

While there is hope when we see legislation that at least names racial disparities, hope when we see people pushing for more accountability toward student outcomes, hope when families have choices in schools, and hope when people donate money toward pre-Kindergarten through 12th grade education, a key rests in the ultimate intentions of any such prerogatives. The question is not, are the intentions good or evil, noble, or nefarious? The question is, will the intentions lead toward social justice, or will they lead toward social reproduction? If we are not clearly intentional about changing the status quo, about moving past a two-track educational system, the tides of business as usual will happily catch any person, foundation, or policy in maintaining it.

Justice by Design aims to further empower educators within the confines of our current landscape. *Justice by Design* proposes one path, not the only path, but a path to intentionally design curriculum oriented toward social justice. It provides educators with a process to backward plan curriculum that leads toward social justice. To begin this process, the next chapter lays out a vision for what "orienting toward social justice" can mean guiding our purpose and ultimately our intentions.

Recap and Moving Forward

Despite the dominant narrative that education is the great equalizer, our educational system in the US is awash with intentions to maintain the status quo of haves and have nots. Given the direction of the floods we have to hold strong intentions to push against the current and move toward the shores of social justice. In the next chapter, we ground in a purpose and vision for social justice, an intention to help set our course.

Chapter 3

Building Intention: Purpose and Vision for Curriculum Oriented Toward Social Justice

We can only see so far, literally and in our collective imaginations. So it's also good to be aware that you may be setting your vision based on the horizon you can see, and as you move towards it, it will change. The gift is, it keeps going. On this planet there are as many horizons as there are places to be (stand, sit, fly, etc.) x 360 degrees x seconds of the day. I am not fluent in math, but that seems to be a pretty massive number of horizons! So hold the vision, and know that as you grow, as you move towards it, the vision will adapt too.

— ADRIENNE MAREE BROWN (2017), SELF IDENTIFIES AS BLACK MIXED RACE, QUEER, SHE/THEY, AND A WRITER. ADDITIONALLY, ON A PERSONAL LEVEL, HER WRITING WAS A HUGE INSPIRATION FOR MUCH OF THIS BOOK AND MY PERSONAL PATH.

Essential Question: What does social justice mean?

Narrative: Equity-Based Missions

I have taught in public district, charter, and residential schools. I have coached teachers in contract alternative, private parochial, and high-performing secular schools. I have taught and coached in rural and urban environments, in general education, Special-Education environments, and in high-performing and low-performing schools. I have worked in schools with a majority of White students, schools with a majority of students of color, schools with racial diversity, schools with an affluent student body, and schools with a majority of students on free and reduced lunches. I have had the privilege over my educational career to be immersed in a variety of school environments.

While contemplating purpose and vision for systems oriented toward social justice, three institutions stand out in my memory.

The first is a federal setting Level IV Emotional and Behavior Disorder (EBD) residential facility in a rural, predominantly White outer-ring suburb of Minneapolis, Minnesota, where I started my career as a pre-service teacher. "Level IV," is a Special Education term for a school site completely separate from a general education school building. For instance, a Level IV EBD facility is one where students with behavioral difficulties too *severe* to be in a regular school building are sent. For example, in our facility we had anywhere from twelve to sixteen students at a given time who were located in the basement of a local clinic.

There are some beautiful Level IV facilities that truly support our youth with significant needs who may require being separated from general education settings for a moment in time. However, in practice, many schools and districts use Level IVs to dump students they feel they no longer want to deal with or have capacity to deal with. In my own experience as a Special Education administrator, I have been at this crossroad and at times supported plans to move a student to a more restrictive setting because of a lack of capacity, training, and support in my building, not because a student truly needed to be separated from her peers. This is a difficult decision I am still grappling with emotionally, processing my feelings of guilt, regret, sadness, and hope that my students were able to find a better fit for their needs.

Sadly, I personally believe there are too few Level IV facilities out there that offer much more than a dumping ground. Truthfully, while I loved the staff and students I worked with at the Level IV facility where I student taught, it was not one of the beautiful exceptions. Consider that the facility was located in a predominantly White district (94 percent White). In the entire district, Black students made up approximately 0.7 percent of students. Put another way, there were roughly twenty Black students districtwide out of over 3,400 students. However, in the restrictive federal setting Level IV EBD program I worked in, two of sixteen students were Black males—that means 10 percent of the Black students were sent to the Level IV, while only 0.4 percent of White students were. *Interesting?* This pattern was not unique to my facility or district; it replicated the story of an overrepresentation of Black boys in Special Education seen across the US—a problem and deficit of a racist system not a problem with Black boys or even overtly bigoted educators.

The staff at my Level IV were all White, but they were not bigoted or hateful toward people of color. The staff were all without fail loving and dedicated to all their students and to transitioning their students back to their mainstream schools as soon as possible, regardless of race or gender or disability or any other marker. Our program director knew students should not be in the restrictive setting for long and worked incredibly hard to ensure three to four students (around 30 percent) were always in transition back to their mainstream district school, a rarity in the world of Level IVs.

However, the staff operated in a racist system where they were taught to ignore racial disparities such as the overrepresentation of Black boys in Special Education. They worked in a system where the educators at the mainstream schools who sent students to our Level IV were taught to ignore the same racial disparities along with their own biases toward dark bodies.

While working there, I made many meaningful connections and had many meaningful conversations with both staff and students, but one conversation was always absent: *Why* was there an extreme overrepresentation of Black boys in our restrictive setting? What is it about our mainstream schools that Black boys are being sent to us at such higher rates than White boys? I use the word *boys* because most of the students in our program were male. And we discussed the overrepresentation of males in our program: fifteen out of sixteen students were male, but we did not discuss race. We did not have a mission or vision that incorporated racial equity,[9] and as such, our conversations and practices followed a colorblind[10] mentality that reinforced racial disparities and White supremacy.

After my pre-service teaching, I went on to work for a public district magnet school in Minneapolis. The school fit all of my criteria for a dream job at the time. As a New Yorker born and raised, being in a city with a racially and socioeconomically diverse population was on the list. Being a young twenty-something-year-old White guy *ready to change the world*, a public school with a meaningful mission was ideal. And being a lover of music, sculpture, painting, drawing, and performing, a focus on the arts was also a plus. In just a fifteen-minute bike ride from my apartment in Minneapolis, I found a racially and socioeconomically diverse interdistrict arts magnet school with a vision intertwining racial equity and the arts. The school was a perfect fit!

---

[9] See page 40-41 for a brief description of the term *racial equity*.
[10] In a color-blind mentality in the US, the dominant group (White folks) perceive that racism is no longer prevalent after the struggles of the Civil Rights Movement or the election of a Black president. In this perspective, people who identify as BIPOC are viewed as hypersensitive or too conscious about race. In color-blind thinking, the belief on the surface is that if everyone simply ignored race, the world would be a better, more equal place—erasing the impact of systems supporting White supremacy and privileges afforded a select few. The goal of color-blind thinking is to minimize racial inequality—to state that racial inequality does not exist and ignore it in an effort to pretend the world is racially equitable. This practice of minimization allows the dominate group in the US to deny current racial inequality claimed by BIPOCs.

BUILDING INTENTION: PURPOSE AND VISION FOR CURRICULUM ORIENTED TOWARD SOCIAL JUSTICE

The fact that the school had one central equity vision felt incredible—and sealed the deal on my desire to work there. Our vision was to use the fine arts with an integration lens for students and staff to provide learning performance, which was "above the race and income demographics."

I taught there for four years. I met my wife, who identifies as a LatinX woman, and mother to my children there. I watched my students grow and learn there. I learned to love my students and their families while there. I learned valuable lessons as an educator on a daily basis. In the building, conversations addressing racial inequity and disparities in our outcomes were commonplace—between staff, between students, between families. However, we never arrived. We never met our equity vision or came close to meeting it. If anything, over the years I spent there, I watched our racial and socioeconomic disparities increase.

We had a vision rooted in equity, but we had no agreed-upon beliefs underpinning our purpose and no road map for how to realize our goals. We had no guidance and no systemwide support. I watched year after year as students I loved—White, Black, and Brown—graduate without the reading, writing, or math skills to make it in college because we lacked rigor and high expectations in our classrooms. Year after year, I watched my students who did make it into college drop out because they were not adequately prepared by us. Ultimately, I felt complicit in perpetuating a two-track system and the myth of opportunity and could not maintain the cognitive dissonance between my actions, our assertions to families, and our outcomes.

For example, the majority of students we served were on free or reduced lunch, meaning they would be considered below the poverty line. As a magnet school, students came from all over the metro area. Because of how systems stratify society in this country, more of our White students came from neighboring, wealthier suburbs, were not as likely to be on free and reduced lunch, and were more likely to make it to and through college, where our Black and Brown students were more likely to come from poorer districts, be on free and reduced lunch, and less likely to make it to and through college. While this was not absolute (I failed many of my White students there just as much as I failed my Black and Brown students), these were general trends, spurred by our low expectations and rigor. I began to see these trends in my second year, and by year three, I began to accept that I was complicit in this system. However, despite knowing our outcomes, I continued to assert to families and students that we would prepare them for college and their dreams because I wanted to believe we could. This led to too much cognitive dissonance and my departure after four years there. While I knew I had to make this choice, it was a hard choice, given my connections to the school, students, families, and staff, but I could only see myself perpetuating inequities if I stayed; I could only see myself as an oppressor if I stayed. So I had to leave.

BUILDING INTENTION: PURPOSE AND VISION FOR CURRICULUM ORIENTED TOWARD SOCIAL JUSTICE

Upon leaving, I was fortunate to become a founding member of a new public charter high school in the same city, a high school that had an equity-based mission, along with a specific equity vision. Our mission was to ensure 100 percent of our students graduated with the leadership and academic skills to graduate college, and our vision was to honor the humanity of all people and actively disrupt systemic inequity in pursuit of an equitable world.

We also had structure and support to realize our goals. We had conversations surrounding racial and socioeconomic disparities on a daily basis with staff and students. Many of our classrooms were spaces filled with truth telling and rigor and love. We created a space where I found myself incredibly connected with staff, students, and families. By the time I left the charter school four years later to help found an alternative Teacher Preparation program, we had not accomplished every aspect of our mission, but we were building toward it.

In my educational career, I have never worked for an institution that has *arrived*; I have never personally taught a class that I would argue accomplished all the goals of social justice. We have not *arrived* as an educational system, and I have not *arrived* as a cisgender White male educator.

But I feel fortunate to have worked in institutions with strong "why's" centered in equity[11] and social justice. While having a strong *why* rooted in social justice does not mean one automatically achieves a just distribution of wealth, opportunities, and privileges, it does not mean we can check the box—justice realized, we have arrived, work done. A strong *why* is a necessary foundation, a starting point for any organization or individual classroom teacher orienting their curriculum toward social justice.

Why Start with Why?

So often as teachers, we jump to what we are going to teach or how we are going to teach it, quickly skimming past *why*. And I get it. I've lived it. As teachers, we know that tomorrow we are going to face a multitude of students, and we need to have something prepared for them. We need our "what" ready to go so we can print, rehearse, adapt, etc.

Ultimately, when we are observed or assessed, people will look at *what* we did and its impact, most likely skimming past *why* we did it. As I have yet to see a teacher observation rubric that details *the why*—and how could an observation tool even begin to tackle *the why* behind our curriculum development and pedagogy?—*the why* is so often unobservable. How can we rate teachers on their purpose, vision, and beliefs in a system that so often requires us to

---

[11] See page 40-41 for a brief description of the term *equity*.

judge and quantify our teachers and their practice in the first place?

It makes sense that we often skim past *the why* of our curriculum development. The system sets us up to skip past *why*.

At its root, *the why* can be defined as our purpose, vision, and beliefs, and skimming past an awareness or analyses of these *whys* too often supports the dominant social order. As we discussed in chapter 2, historically, *the why* behind so many of our educational materials and practices in the US has been social reproduction, maintaining the status quo of haves and have nots. But part of any design for social justice requires unlearning. We need to unlearn this habit; we need to spend time focusing on our *why*: our personal *why*, the purpose behind our curriculum development, the vision we set our curriculum, and the beliefs that underlie our decisions.

Without a clear analysis of *why*, we can be caught by the traps of textbooks replete with heroic depictions of Christopher Columbus (a false narrative created in the 1950s by Democrats to assimilate Italians into Whiteness and win Italian votes) instead of honesty around Columbus's genocide of native peoples and exploitation of the Americas. Without an analysis of why, we can be caught teaching that science has always been about objective truth[12] and facts, instead of the reality that science (as most

---

[12] See page 86-87 for a description of how "objectivity" has been used to oppress people.

institutions in the US) has at numerous points been contorted to reinforce the domination, colonization, and exploitation of people who have been marginalized. Without an analysis of why, we can be caught teaching math by memorizing procedures versus deeply understanding problem solving—setting students up for a lifetime of complying to the procedure and not working on creative problem solving. Our educational materials and pedagogies are so often designed for social reproduction. We need to be intentional about our purpose to ensure we do not replicate more of the same. Intention begins with *why*.

Good design is always rooted in *why*. Rooting our work in *why* goes beyond teaching. In 2009, Simon Sinek, who professionally identifies as an optimist, sent rippling effects through countless organizations as he laid out his Golden Circle to explain how great leaders inspire action. The heart of his model depicts how knowing *why* we do what we do can be the key to unlocking success and inspiration.

In the realm of social justice, *the why*, *the how*, and *the what* are all important, though an alignment to *the why* is paramount. Without alignment to a why oriented toward social justice, a potentially liberating practice can be oppressive. Take teachers who requires their students to raise a silent hand in class because students must conform to the teacher's will versus teachers who requires their students to raise a silent hand because they want to create consistent community signals and routines to support every student's voice, or because they love each student and believe this expectation is key for their future success in a violent educational system. Rooting our curriculum and pedagogies in our purpose, vision, and belief, that is, in our *why*, is why this book dedicates the first four chapters to building context for *the why*.

Vision and Purpose for Curriculum Oriented Toward Social Justice

Let's start by defining *justice*. As the acclaimed author and feminist activist bell hooks, who self identifies as an intellectual, feminist theorist, cultural critic, artist, writer, and Black woman, poses in the documentary, *Occupy Love* (Ripper, 2012), "What is justice? The heart of it is really longing for people to be able to grow and develop freely in a positive and constructive way." Building on this, a brief google search provides a definition of *social* justice: Social justice is *justice in terms of the distribution of wealth, opportunities, and privileges within a society* (Lexico, 2020). Put together, social justice could be thought of as redistributing wealth, opportunities, and privileges so that people are able to grow and develop freely in a positive and constructive way.

In the US, we do not have a just distribution of wealth, opportunities, and privileges. We have never had a just distribution of wealth, opportunities, and privileges since our founding, due to oppressive systems built into our foundation that have blossomed and adapted over the past four hundred years. In the US, the wealthiest 1 percent of households own more wealth than the bottom 90 percent combined (Wolff, 2017). Women make 20 percent less than men, with Hispanic women making almost 60 percent less than White men (EPI, 2017). Black men are more than five times as likely to be incarcerated than White men, despite the same propensity for criminal offenses (The Sentencing Project, 2016). In the US, 32 percent of classrooms with predominantly students of color never have access to grade-level rigorous classwork, compared to 12 percent of classrooms with predominantly White students (TNTP, 2018). There is not a just distribution of wealth, opportunities, and privileges based on race, class, gender, and several other identity markers and intersections. A classroom oriented toward social justice should strive to bring about a just distribution of wealth, opportunities, and privileges.

In a widely accepted more detailed definition for social justice, Lee Anne Bell (Adams, Bell & Griffin, 1997), who identities as White, cisgender, female, temporarily able-bodied, gentile, working class to upper middle class, retired professor moving into elder status agewise writes,

> *We believe that social justice is both a process and a goal. The goal of social justice is the full and equal participation of all groups in a society that is mutually shaped to meet their needs. Social justice includes a vision of society that is mutually shaped to meet their needs. Social justice includes a vision of society in which the distribution of resources is equitable and all members are physically and*

> *psychologically safe and secure. We envision a society in which individuals are both self-determining (able to develop their full capacities) and interdependent (capable of interacting democratically with others). Social justice involves social actors who have a sense of their own agency as well as a sense of social responsibility toward and with others, their society, and the broader world in which we live. These are conditions we wish not only for our own society but also for every society in our interdependent global community...*
> *We realize that developing a social justice process in a society and world steeped in oppression is no simple feat. For this reason, we need clear ways to define and analyze oppression so that we can understand how it operates at individual, cultural, and institutional levels, historically and in the present. (Adams, Bell, & Griffin, 1997)*

A vision for social justice includes full and equal participation of all groups in society working together, where members feel safe and self-determined, and where there is an equitable distribution of resources and opportunities. To achieve this vision, social justice requires a just *how*. In other words, social justice is both a process and a goal because one cannot achieve a social justice vision through domination, oppression, and compliance, but only through socially just actions.

One key word mentioned in Bell's definition that should be elucidated is "equitable." Dr. David Stovall asserts that, "Equity? is really talking about redistribution... When we talk about equity, we have to talk about who has historically been denied opportunity, and then how are those opportunities denied in real time, currently" (Hindery, 2018). Many groups have been excluded from access to resources and opportunities based on several identity markers such as sex, race, and class. Lack of access can also be compounded based on having several identities that have been marginalized. Equity is about redistribution to bring about a just distribution of wealth, opportunities, and privileges. The term *racial equity* is used to highlight the fact that a key identity marker often taught to be ignored by White supremacy is race.

The national racial justice organization Seeking Educational Equity and Diversity (SEED) describes a vision and purpose for social justice, building off of Bell's definition by providing us with a vivid metaphor that I will repeat numerous times throughout this book. SEED provides the metaphor of cages and nests. These metaphors have helped me set a personal vision I can picture for orienting curriculum toward social justice. In describing this metaphor, the co-director of SEED, educator, researcher, capacity builder, and Taiwanese American, Jondue Chen (2018), states,

> *What makes a nest a nest and a cage a cage? Both are constructed realities. Yet one of them is self-determined and the other is segregated. Both can be a home. Yet one allows for near infinite future possibilities and the other represents only a monotonous and controlled existence. In seeking to be our whole selves and in just relationship with others, we at SEED see our identities, our cultures, and our communities as our nests... [while] cages can serve as an effective metaphor for systemic oppression, with each wire of the cage representing one aspect of sexism or racism or any other-ism that entraps us... Revealing systemic oppression and moving towards tearing down our birdcages has been and remains*

central to our work in SEED... Yet if all we see ourselves as is cage crushers, is this justice enough?.... For a bird to be its whole self, is it enough to simply be without a cage? We would argue no. A bird on its own would soon die or die eventually, without a future generation. It is the possibility of building one's own nest, and of forming just relationships with others in the same or neighboring nest that we see what is possible for the bird in the present and in its future. To deprive a bird of its nest, in fact, is a form of caging, for it denies the bird its connection to its past and its future. Similarly, consider what it means that some birds move into the abandoned homes of other birds and that some birds push out other birds. What does it mean to appreciate and learn from other cultures in a respectful way versus appropriating or colonizing the work of others?

bell hooks (2003) reiterates this dual vision and purpose in *Teaching Community: A Pedagogy of Hope*, noting that educators working toward social justice must voice both opposition to dominating forces that stifle freedom and voice hope. Curriculums oriented toward social justice should facilitate both the deconstruction of intersecting systems of oppression *and* the development of loving, self-determined, and empowered individuals. Classrooms oriented toward social justice should center issues of racism, classism, sexism, transphobia, ableism, and any other ism, as well as center counternarratives and hope. To facilitate social justice in our curricular design and educational intentions we must support our students to both crush cages *and* build nests.

Social justice can mean and should mean more than one thing: we cannot get trapped by simplistic either/or ideology. For example, we cannot get trapped into thinking either you think like me or you are against me. We must accept the limits of our own understanding and therefore refuse simplistic binaries. To realize social justice, we must embrace a both/and mindset (more on this in chapter 5).

"Both/and" thinking allows us to add several dimensions to our *why*. For me, the purpose for writing curriculum oriented toward social justice is about supporting a just redistribution of resources, opportunities, and privileges, naming oppressive systems, crushing cages, building nests, *and* self-healing. "Both/and" thinking, also referred to in this book as *"yes, and"* thinking supports a complex *why* rooted in social justice.

Sample Vision and Purpose Statements

To aid us in intentionality, we should create personal purpose and vision statements for our curriculum design. By understanding the complex depth of social justice, equity, redistribution, goals and processes, nests, and cages we can begin to construct purpose and vision statements that are broad, concise, meaningful, and useful in guiding our work toward social justice. Below are two examples, touchpoints, for your own purpose and vision statements to evolve.

Purpose Statement: To build curriculum to critically examine our world, support a just redistribution of wealth, opportunities, and privileges and provides healing from the disease of colonization and domination.

Vision Statement: To create rigorous units and lesson plans that foster deconstructing intersectional systems of oppression and empower loving, self-determined scholars oriented toward positive relationships and connectedness.

Recap and Moving Forward

What is your purpose and vision for curriculum oriented toward social justice? How does your personal definition of social justice intertwine into your purpose and vision statements? Are you prepared to let your vision adapt with the moving horizon? How do you think your purpose, vision, and beliefs will affect the outcomes of your curriculum? In the next chapter, we will review the importance of belief, focusing on one belief in particular.

Chapter 4

Believing: Love Is Justice

Never forget that justice is what love looks like in public.

— CORNEL WEST, SELF-IDENTIFIED PROMINENT AND PROVOCATIVE DEMOCRATIC INTELLECTUAL, BLACK MAN.

Essential Question: What is real love?

Narrative: The Stories We Tell Ourselves

I have made up countless stories to tell myself. When I was in elementary and middle school, I struggled academically and considered myself overweight. Back then, I consistently told myself, "I am the fat kid; I don't look in mirrors or take pictures, and I don't have a lot of friends." I still remember hating mirrors, and only now can I really look back and smile at the few pictures of myself that exist from those years. Back then, I consistently told myself, "I am the worst at classwork and tests, I can't do homework, I can't read, but I am great at art." Not surprisingly, I almost never did my homework, I pretended not to pay attention to avoid being called on to read, and I generally earned very poor grades in everything but art class. I consistently told myself, "While I am not good at school, I am a fighter. I won't start fights, but if anyone picks on me or one of my few friends, I will fight them and beat them." And not surprisingly, I got into a lot of fights in those years and spent a lot of time in the principal's office. My fighting culminated in breaking another student's jaw while at school, and I was subsequently kicked out of my 6th-grade alma mater. Interestingly, the story my mother tells herself is that she chose to remove me from my school in 6th grade because they didn't know how to teach a kid with learning disabilities and ADHD.

The stories we tell ourselves have power. Sharon Salzberg (2017) writes in *Real Love,* we are innately programmed to create order, mental organization, and cohesive narratives. In this regard, Salzberg argues the stories we tell ourselves are our anchors; they inform us of who we are, what matters most, what our potential is, and what our lives are all about.

When I was in elementary and middle school, my stories were filled with the narratives of someone who was not capable in school, someone who wanted to run from himself, and someone who did not love himself. Now, my story goes something like, "I was the kid with learning disabilities who got kicked out of school but went to college, got his degrees to become a teacher, and now teaches teachers. I am the person who overcame certain struggles with support, privilege, and love." Ironically, I now love mirrors and selfies, maybe even a little too much, but for me it all comes with loving myself. Not a narcissistic love. It is a love that recognizes my faults as areas for continual growth rather than pretending I am perfect. A love that recognizes my unearned advantages and privileges in life and strives to address these wrongs. My personal love holds me accountable to be better and is always forgiving when I fail. I believe I am on the path toward real love.

Belief

Our beliefs will always impact our outcomes, regardless of our intention. Don Miguel Ruiz (1997), renowned spiritual teacher and author from Mexico writes in the, *The Four Agreements: A Practical Guide to Personal Freedom (A Toltec Wisdom Book)* that, "The belief system is like a Book of Law that rules our mind. Without question, whatever is in that Book of Law, is our truth. We base all of our judgments according to the Book of Law, even if these judgments go against our own inner nature. Even moral laws like the Ten Commandments are programmed into our mind in the process of domestication. One by one, all these agreements go into the Book of Law, and these agreements rule our dream." To dream of social justice, we must recognize and address our personal beliefs.

And that takes effort and work.

What do you believe White students are capable of? What do you believe Black and Brown and Asian Students are capable of? What do you believe Native and Indigenous students are capable of? What do you believe students with disabilities are capable of?

What do you believe students from different linguistic backgrounds are capable of? What do you believe ultra-wealthy students are capable of? What do you believe students from generational poverty are capable of? What do you believe teachers are capable of? What do you believe school administrators are capable of? What do you believe policy writers are capable of? What do you believe you are capable of?

Do you believe we are all capable of change and growth?

We all have unique life experiences that will affect our personal beliefs, our *Book of Law*. Addressing the beliefs that hinder orienting curriculum toward social justice is important self-work. To aid in this work, I propose laying a universal foundation for orienting curriculum toward social justice: a belief in real love and its power.

Real Love

There is a reason the narrative I chose to share for this chapter is about me and not directly about my teaching or my students. Love, real love, begins with self-love, and social justice needs real love to flourish. Does social justice also need love for our students, families, and fellow educators? Yes, and real love that brings enough sustainability to love others indefinitely, begins with self-love.

Sharon Salzberg (2017), author and teacher of Buddhist meditation in the West writes in *Real Love*, "Real love comes with a powerful recognition that we are fully alive and whole, despite our wounds or our fears or our loneliness. It is a state where we allow ourselves to be seen clearly by ourselves and by others, and in turn, we offer clear seeing to the world around us. It is a love that heals." To pull out a key idea, real love starts with self-love, which allows us to see ourselves and others clearly. Self-love allows us to look honestly in the mirror and see our potential for growth, regardless of any of our faults, just as much as it allows us to love our students and see their potential for growth.

Without self-love, it is difficult to sustain love for anyone else, though not impossible. Salzberg notes, "I have never believed that you must completely love yourself first before you can love another. I know many people who are hard on themselves, yet love their friends and family deeply and are loved in return—though they might have difficulty in receiving that love. But it's hard to sustain love for others over the long haul until we have a sense of inner abundance and sufficiency."

Work toward social justice is work that needs to be done over the long haul. To cultivate real love in abundance and sufficiency to love others over the long haul, we can use positive self-narration, that is, tell our personal stories through a positive and forgiving lens, incorporate loving kindness and mindfulness into our daily routines, and believe that we are worthy of love. At the core of a belief in love, I hold these words from Sharon Salzberg (2017):

BELIEVING: LOVE IS JUSTICE

You deserve all the love in the world.
You do not have to earn love.
You simply have to exist.

Yes, and we can turn these words towards our students, to read...

Your students deserve all the love in the world.
Your students do not have to earn love.
Your students simply have to exist.

Yes, and we can turn these words toward our students' families, fellow educators, and even educational policy makers.

The Vietnamese Buddhist monk Thich Nhat Hanh, shared back in 1975 that: "The way must be in you; the destination also must be in you and not somewhere else in space or time. If that kind of self-transformation is being realized in you, you will arrive." (hooks, 2000b)

While orienting curriculum toward social justice is about reaching a societal destination together, it also requires a personal destination with continual self-work that begins with self-love. In turn, loving ourselves supports our community just as a loving community can support our personal growth. Thich Nhat Hanh shared in a conversation with bell hooks in 2000, "We can't expect... love to come from outside of us. We should ask the question whether we are capable of loving ourselves as well as others... the question is whether we are practicing loving ourselves? Because loving ourselves means loving our community. When we are capable of loving ourselves, nourishing ourselves properly, not intoxicating ourselves, we are already protecting and nourishing society. Because in the moment when we are able to smile, to look at ourselves with compassion, our world begins to change." (hooks, 2000b)

In turn, Thich Nhat Hanh shares that, "If love is there in the community, if we've been nourished by the harmony in the community, then we will never move away from love." Loving our community means loving ourselves, and in turn our community supports our love.

When I look back at my life experiences, real love did not come naturally to me despite being a cisgender White man from a socioeconomically stable family background in a larger society (the US) where national narratives are filled with false stock stories that demonstrate those with my identity markers have high self-worth at the cost of those with different identity markers than my own. The testament of those with several marginalized identities and prolonged adversities to continue to survive and thrive day in and day out is a testament to real love. There is real love to be found in all communities from the most marginalized and oppressed to the most disproportionately advantaged. As an educator, it is crucial to lead with love, bring real love into our classrooms and curriculum, and create space where self-love can flourish for all.

Love and Teaching

Parker Palmer (1998), a Quaker elder, educator, activist, and founder and senior partner emeritus of the Center for Courage & Renewal, writes on the intersection of love and teaching that:

> *As good teachers weave the fabric that joins them with students and subjects, the heart is the loom on which the threads are tied, the tension is held, the shuttle flies, and the fabric is stretched tight. Small wonder, then, that teaching tugs at the heart, opens the heart, even breaks the heart— and the more one loves teaching, the more heartbreaking it can be. The courage to teach is the courage to keep one's heart open in those very moments when the heart is asked to hold more than it is able so that teacher and students and subject can be woven into the fabric of community that learning, and living, require.*

To truly teach and build a community we need love, and the courage to love as loving opens us up to heartbreak.

In moving from self-love toward loving our students, hooks (2003) writes, "In All About Love: New Visions I defined love as a combination of care, commitment, knowledge, responsibility, respect, and trust. All these factors work interdependently. They are a core foundation of love irrespective of the relational context. Even though there is a difference between romantic love and the love between teacher and pupil, these core aspects must be present for love to be love."

To personalize hooks's framework:

- ❖ Do you truly take care of yourself?
- ❖ Do you commit to being better?

- ❖ Have you honestly looked in the mirror to better know yourself and your *book of law*?
- ❖ Do you show yourself respect?
- ❖ Do you trust yourself and intuitions?

We can also use hooks's framework to continue looking in the mirror with real love, self-love, honest love together by asking:

- ❖ Do you truly care about and feel empathy for your students?
- ❖ Do you put in the extra time commitment needed to redevelop your curriculum and provide meaningful feedback?
- ❖ Do you really *know* your students, their families, their desires, their strengths, and their struggles?
- ❖ Do you hold yourself and your students to high expectations?
- ❖ Do you always show your students culturally responsive[13] respect?
- ❖ Do you trust *your* future to your students?

Can you forgive yourself and adapt if you are not able to answer yes with vast details and emotional input to each of the above questions?

hooks (2003) goes on to write in *Teaching Community: A Pedagogy of Hope* that when "principles of love form the basis of

---

[13] Cultural competency is the ability to understand, communicate with, and effectively interact with people across cultures.

teacher-pupil interaction the mutual pursuit of knowledge creates the conditions for optimal learning. Teachers, then, are learning while teaching and students are learning and sharing knowledge." Sharon Salzburg (2017) reiterates this process by stating, "Our minds are changed when our hearts are engaged." Love allows all members in your community to engage, learn, and grow, including ourselves.

Without love, we open the potential for a lack of empathy, lack of commitment, lack of understanding, lack of accountability, and lack of respect and trust. Without love, we open the door to oppression and domination. Love and social justice are synonymous in many ways. Again, while every individual will bring a unique and personal life story filled with countless beliefs that may support and orient curriculum toward social justice, there is one belief that I *believe* should be universal: that is a belief in Real Love and its power.

Love and Justice

As noted throughout this book, I think it is important to center the voices of those who have been most marginalized in our society. There is an irony here given my identity markers as author, but in moving toward both/and, I hope I am still able to center the voices of women who identify as Black, Indigenous, and People of Color (BIPOC) while writing this. This is particularly important here as my personal experience dictates that while I can find Real Love, I will never have the same embodied understanding of Real Love intertwined with social justice as those who have been most marginalized in society.

Let's draw on words from Ellen Vanden Branden (2020) to better elucidate this. Ellen was my first guide into the world of *Understanding by Design* reflected throughout this book. She is an incredible teacher, teacher of teachers, and friend. She identifies as a Korean-international, transracial adoptee, and cis female. Ellen was an accountability reviewer for this book, and in her feedback, she shared these powerful words that help to give context for why it is so important that we center the voices of those most marginalized, especially in the realm of love and social justice:

> *As I read this section, I'm reminded of a powerful lecture I heard by Jonathan Rosa at the Hollyhock Fellowship Program. I think this section needs to name that one of the goals of colonization is to make you feel self-hatred if you are not a member of the dominant group in order to justify your inferiority. Love is radical justice, especially when the system wants you to hate yourself for the system to gain and function as it was designed. The genocide and forced schooling of the indigenous people of this land was a violent and systematic attempt to deem an entire people and culture unworthy. The enslavement of Africans was only 'justifiable' by creating a narrative of dehumanization from its inception. And Real Love is a radical reclamation of worth, culture, celebration, etc. If we teach for social and specifically, racial justice, I believe white educators need to cultivate self-love so as not to perpetuate these harmful histories onto the communities they serve, and BIPOC educators get to radically reclaim their love for themselves.*

Love may mean different things to different groups or individuals, and real love may require more or less resiliency depending on one's identities and histories, but love is always power.

Adriene Maree Brown (2017) writes in *Emergent Strategy*, "If love were the central practice of a new generation of organizers and spiritual leaders, it would have a massive impact on what was considered organizing. If the goal was to increase the love, rather than winning or dominating a constant opponent, I think we could actually imagine liberation from constant oppression."

Looking historically, bell hooks (2003) describes in *Teaching Community: A Pedagogy of Hope* that she began to understand the connection between love and ending domination by realizing that a love ethic was central to the power in anti-racist civil rights struggles in the 1960s, arguably one of the most revolutionary movements for social justice in the world. Love is central to liberation and social justice—domination and hate can never lead to true freedom, domination and hate can only replicate more of the same.

To think about this in terms of the classroom, Dr. Bettina Love (2019), award-winning author whose writing, research, teaching, and activism meet at the intersection of race, education, abolition, and Black joy, and who identifies as a queer Black woman, describes in *We Want to Do More than Survive*, that teachers who believe their students are animals, based on characteristics such as race or family national origin, cannot teach their students with love. Teachers cannot support dehumanizing rhetoric and hate for students' identities and still teach those students with kindness, care, and see the beauty in their students' differences. If we teach with hate, we can only strive for domination. If we teach without love, we can only oppress. But when we can see ourselves and our students as emotional beings, we are able to build a foundation of love with all the opportunities for trust, risk-taking, growth, and connection. All the opportunities made possible by love.

Adrienne Maree Brown (2017) goes on to write, "One thing I have observed: When we are engaged in acts of love, we humans are at our best and most resilient." Love can lead us to be better and often reshape our entire lives for our partners, our children, and our elders. Love allows us to forge on in our classrooms, sometimes with broken hearts, limited prep time, too few supplies, or a lack of support. Love allows us to look in the mirror with compassion when we fail.

While love can open us up to unimagined possibilities and unimagined heartbreak, Real Love allows us to forgive—forgive ourselves, our coworkers, our students. And we can always find love in heartbreak because the hurt, both physical and mental pain, demonstrate our humanity. Love may mean different things to different groups or individuals, real love may require more or less resiliency depending on one's identities, but love is always power.

Martin Luther King, Jr. (1967) reflected in his last presidential address to the Southern Christian Leadership Conference on August 16, 1967 on the true power of love:

> ...*Now, we got to get this thing right. What is needed is a realization that power without love is reckless and abusive, and that love without power is sentimental and anemic. Power at its best is love implementing the demands of justice, and justice at its best is love correcting everything that stands against love....*
>
> *And I say to you, I have also decided to stick with love, for I know that love is ultimately the only answer to mankind's problems. (Yes) And I'm going to talk about it everywhere I go... I'm talking about a strong, demanding love. (Yes) For I have seen too much hate. (Yes) I've seen too much hate on the faces of sheriffs in the South. (Yeah) I've seen hate on the faces of too many Klansmen and too many White Citizens Councilors in the South to want to hate, myself, because every time I see it, I know that it does something to their faces and their personalities, and I say to myself that hate is too great a burden to bear. (Yes, that's right) I have decided to love. [applause] If you are seeking the highest good, I think you can find it through love. And the beautiful thing is that we aren't moving wrong when we do it, because John was right, God is love. (Yes) He who hates does not know God, but he who loves has the key that unlocks the door to the meaning of ultimate reality.*

I do not have the words to summarize or build on or explain Martin Luther King Jr's assertions, but I will repeat one line: "Power at its best is love implementing the demands of justice, and justice at its best is love correcting everything that stands against love."

Recap and Moving Forward

Love is power. Love is Justice. God is Love. And Real Love starts when you look in the mirror. "You deserve all the love in the world. You do not have to earn love. You simply have to exist" (Salzberg, 2020). *Yes, and...* Your students deserve all the love in the world. Your students do not have to earn love. Your students simply have to exist. Believe in love.

Part II

The How

Chapter 5

Do Your Self-Work

Teaching holds a mirror to the soul. If I am willing to look in that mirror, and not run from what I see, I have a chance to gain self-knowledge—and knowing myself is as crucial to good teaching as knowing my students and my subject... In fact, knowing my students and my subject depends heavily on self-knowledge. When I do not know myself, I cannot know who my students are. I will see them through a glass darkly, in the shadows of my unexamined life—and when I cannot see them clearly I cannot teach them well. When I do not know myself, I cannot know my subject—not at the deepest levels of embodied, personal meaning. I will know it only abstractly, from a distance, a congeries of concepts as far removed from the world as I am from personal truth.

— PARKER PALMER, *THE COURAGE TO TEACH* (1998).

Essential Question: What values and principles will shape your personal reflections, beliefs, and worldview?

Narrative: Nepotism

I love working with my family. Whether my actual family, or friends I consider family. People often find it hard to believe that my wife, Rocky, and I both love working together. We love commuting together, packing our lunch together, and dropping our kids off together. It makes work feel more like home. Maybe it has to do with the fact we first met while working together in a school. To this day, my thinking has even spread, because I don't just enjoy working with my wife but my entire family.

Several years ago, when I started a new job to help found a charter high school in Minneapolis, it was only a matter of months before I convinced both Rocky and Rocky's sister to apply to work at the fledgling school with me.

In our first year, we were only a staff of eighteen. Students were supposed to call us by our last names, and I often used the same naming convention for my peers. So, when I saw my sister-in-law at work I'd say, "Hello Ms. Xochihua." And given how small we were, I saw her quite often.

One day, Ms. X, my sister-in-law, asked Rocky, "What the hell is wrong with your husband? Why does he act like he doesn't know me at work?" And she was right. It was beyond merely going by last names. My whole demeanor was different at work, my communication style was different, and it was as if I said, "*Hello Ms. Xochihua,*" through a darkened and foggy glass barrier. I was disconnected from my authentic self.

Rocky would tell her sister, "I know. That is work Ian. He acts like he doesn't know any of us. Don't take offense. It's how he was trained." For a time, I was proud of my ability to transform at work and leave my authentic self at home.

To return to my preservice student teaching at a Level IV Emotional and Behavioral (EBD) facility in a rural suburb of Minneapolis (see chapter 3), I taught under my mentor, Ms.

Anderson, a White woman. Ms. Anderson was incredible. She had been a teacher for the past thirty years and just had a way with students. She especially loved working with the toughest students who came into the program, and they loved working with her. Her support was a large reason that so many of the students there transferred back to their local schools relatively quickly for a Level IV EBD program.

The program used the Boys Town Method, a schoolwide system with a complex set of positive reinforcers, negative reinforcers, punishments, procedures, success stories, and its fair share of questionable practices for a classroom oriented toward social justice. One Boys Town redirection procedure I quickly learned involved reciting the following lines when a student was displaying "problem behavior": "Right now you are doing X, you should do Y because of [insert reason]."

As students approximate the desired behavior, "Y" in this case, you shower them with more and more positive reinforcements in the form of effective praise statements, smiles, or tokens. If they don't approximate the desired behavior, you continue repeating those lines with as little emotional affect as possible. Alongside such procedures, I also learned how to position myself physically to reduce tension and how to maintain a constant tone and volume level. At first, these procedures and modes of being felt mechanical, but in time, they became more and more internalized and eventually naturalized.

In particular, I naturalized reducing my emotional affect in front of students whether in my tone, body language, or words. I internalized the idea that if I showed my emotions, such as frustration and anger, I might trigger students and escalate a given situation. While I believe there is truth in this statement, I took this idea to an extreme—suppressing most of my emotions and ultimately suppressing myself while teaching. I also found this suppression at work to fit perfectly with the dominant narrative I was taught and I believed growing up, the narrative that we don't bring our emotions out in public, and we apologize when we accidentally display emotions.

Fast forward six years to working with my sister-in-law, and I naturally became a different person at work. One with completely different mannerisms, language, and a way of being far removed from my authentic self outside of work.

I thought that this was good teaching. What I was supposed to be doing. And it seemed to fit perfectly with countless stock narratives of emotional distancing in White-normed institutions. I missed most of what Ms. Anderson was actually doing in her classroom.

She loved her students. She embodied her emotions, most notably love, and was therefore able to connect with her students emotionally. That was in large part why her students trusted her, accepted her pushes, and made such huge strides with her. She said and did the "Boys Town" procedural things, but what she really did, what really made the difference, can't be captured in a set of "procedures."

Another educator I have been privileged to work with who rivaled Ms. Anderson's ability to call in the most difficult and disconnected students is Rocky. Give Rocky a room full of students who feel they don't matter at school, and she will have her entire class in tears speaking their truths, being vulnerable, and supporting each other's growth in minutes. She has a gift. I try to take notes every time I watch her work with students, but I know I miss most of what she's really doing, because it isn't generally about words and actions; it goes to deeper feelings and beliefs. So when she gives me advice as to how to connect with students, I listen.

After my sister-in-law's observation of my transformation into a robot at work, Rocky told me, "You really do need to be more yourself at work…"

Rocky taught me to bring my authentic self to my classroom. To let go of the robot. To let people in and make them feel connected. It has taken me years to realize how to be my authentic self without being viewed as unprofessional or emotional or lazy. I mean, I do like to wear tracksuits day in and day out. I like to slouch to the maximum degree possible in my chair and rest every bone in my body every time I sit down. I swear. I argue with the passion of a New Yorker born and raised. I manifest many behaviors that are not always viewed as "professional" or "teacher like," in the context of White-normed schools.

But bringing my authentic self to work doesn't mean I need to show up in tracksuits from the 90s sporting my Adidas shell toes. It doesn't mean I should yell down the school hallway like I'm yelling to my daughter upstairs in her bedroom, and it definitely doesn't mean I should let my anger get the best of me in front of students, or worse, toward students. I believe bringing my authentic self to work truly means I should let my love shine at work, and my classroom should feel like a home, not a personal home where I walk around in a towel, because it is a shared space and that would be weird and inappropriate. It should feel like a shared home, where I need to give up personal comforts to co-create a space with my students where we all feel at home. Bringing my authentic self also extends to my curriculum. It means I will teach what I believe to be meaningful. I will personalize our shared learning, and I will reinforce others to bring their authentic selves and thrive in a shared *homeroom*.

I spent too many years of my life hiding my authentic self. From omitting or neglecting to acknowledge my racial, class, and bisexual identities at various points due to shame or guilt, to avoiding my literal reflection in the mirror because of my weight, to pretending I could read when I couldn't. When orienting our classrooms toward social justice, we need to start with an honest look in the mirror, to understand and bring our authentic selves into the light along with our students, our curriculum, and our practices, creating an environment where we all matter and we all feel connected. And that might mean unlearning, as we grow and fail and grow on our journey.

Part II: The How

Part II of this book is about translating our *why* into a set of actionable values and principles to operate on. Our *hows* are the values and principles that guide how to bring curriculum oriented toward social justice to life. Sinek (2009) notes that for our values and principles to be most effective, they should be descriptive actionable statements. For example, he writes, "It's not 'integrity,' it's 'always do the right thing.' It's not 'innovation,' it's 'look at the problem from a different angle.'" Articulating our social-justice-minded values as descriptive actionable statements gives us guidance when creating curriculum oriented toward social justice that minimizes bias and supports deconstructing cages (oppressive systems) and building nests (self-empowerment).

Throughout Part II, I briefly review a series of values and principles worded as actionable statements. By nature, many of these values and principles have overlapping characteristics. Still, given that the list of values and principles is long, I have divided the list into three more manageable-sized chapters. To do this, I attempted to categorize a large number of values and principles into three overarching "how" categories: (A) Do Your Self-Work, (B) Nurture Interdependence, and (C) Stay Grounded.

These are not truly discrete categories; in reality, there are no clear borders between the values and principles listed in this book. In full transparency, I divided the list into three separate categories because when I put the full list into a single chapter, it was way too long and boring to read, even though I only cover brief reviews.

Now, when I say brief, I mean I have attempted to condense lifelong studies into a few paragraphs and quotes. However, each value and principle will naturally guide you toward other authors to explore who can add considerable depth and ultimately lead you to more authors in a cycle of important self-work. To preview, the values and principles listed over the next three chapters are drawn from visionaries, leaders, and educators like Bettina Love, Adrienne Maree Brown, bell hooks, Paulo Freire, and Lisa Delpit to name a few. I thoroughly implore you to read their work and the authors they lead you to before completing this book, especially Dr. Love, Brown, Delpit, and hooks—who as women of color we should all follow on the path toward liberation.

I should also note, while the values and principles listed here draw on the visionary work of prolific activists for social justice, this list is not *the* definitive list, or even *a* definitive list, this is not an exhaustive list, this does not need to be your list… You might be asking at this point, "Why should I even read this?"

For me, this is an evolving list that captures my understanding at this moment in time, an understanding I know will adapt over the coming years as I am called in, called out, to learn and grow. I hope it acts as a starting point, or checkpoint, for your personal list of guiding values and principles for orienting curriculum toward social justice. Let's get started…

Do Your Self-Work

Our vision of the world is always impacted by the lens through which we see. Depending on the lens we are looking through, what we see will change. If we are looking through sunglasses, the world looks one way; if we are looking through binoculars, the world looks another. Besides our physical lenses we all, also, have cultural lenses through which we view the world.

How a person makes sense of the world and processes information is the result of the lens through which they see the world. Our lenses help provide answers to big questions: Who has value? What is freedom? And what is important? They also answer more micro-questions: How do you choose your friends? How important is school? What is normal? The answers to these questions and more form our worldview.

Reflecting on your personal beliefs, your lens and your worldview are crucial to understanding the self, which is crucial to designing curriculum oriented toward social justice. This is difficult work. This is important work. This is self-work. In this chapter, we review five values and principles directly related to critical self-reflection.

1. Be Authentic

Essential Question: How do you move from being a gracious host where your students must still be granted entrance/acceptance into your classroom to building a home *with* your students?

The answer to this question relies on authenticity, but you won't actually find the answer here. I can't answer this for you. We all have to do our own work, cultivate our own understanding of self at our deepest most essential levels. For me, as stated in the opening narrative, being authentic in the classroom does not mean I wear tracksuits from the 90s to work every day (Though I wouldn't mind). It doesn't mean I yell to students across the hall like I am sitting at home yelling to my daughter in the other room—for me, these are more superficial aspects of my authentic self (though that may be different for you and your students). Being authentic in the classroom means I have looked in the mirror honestly. It means I am constantly analyzing my biases, trying to see my students clearly, trying to understand my subject clearly and how I relate to it. For example, I do not teach about White supremacy as a concept in a book or set of definitions or stories experienced by other people; I personalize it. I teach about

White supremacy from my lived experience and encourage my students to understand it through their personal lived experiences.

There is no clear dictionary.com definition for being an authentic educator, but Kreber et al. (2007) has done considerable research and work trying to elucidate the concept to underscore its importance in education. The researchers break down being an authentic educator into the following parts:

1. Being genuine
2. Becoming more self-aware
3. Being defined by one's self rather than by others' expectations
4. Bringing parts of oneself into interactions with students
5. Critically reflecting on self, others, relationships, and context

Kreber et al. (2007) go on to add that authenticity, most importantly, has a moral dimension to it, and ultimately, being authentic guides us to the pivotal question: "Is this in the important interest of learners?"

Let's pause on this definition for a second, because a five-point definition with a bonus moral-based question means we got a lot to unpack. In the first part of the definition by Kreber et al. (2007), we have what I naturally gravitate toward when I hear authenticity: being "genuine" or "oneself." For me, this could mean wearing a tracksuit from the 90s just as much as it could mean allowing myself to have emotions in the workplace. Now, let's look at what Kreber et. al. mean by, critically reflecting on self, others, relationships, and context.

To be genuine, we must understand ourselves; to understand ourselves, we must critically reflect on ourselves. Since we exist in the context of relationships to others, systems, and our environment, in order to critically examine ourselves, we must also critically examine our relationships to others, our place within systems, and our environments. A key word in this is *critical*, meaning an analysis of both merits and faults. It is through a critical lens that we get closer to the *morality*, dimension of authenticity noted by Kreber et al. (2007). It is being critical of ourselves, others, our relationships, and our environments that leads us to the pivotal and moral question: Is this subject matter in the important interest of learners? Being authentic means being critical of who we are, which leads us to be critical of what we teach.

In working to better understand myself, I try to constantly reflect on my beliefs, feelings, thoughts, and past actions in context. The narratives within this book have provided a great opportunity for just that—uncovering both personal merits and faults embedded in my past. Take, for example, my opening narrative from chapter 1: "My First Year Teaching." While reflecting on my first year teaching Kayci, I critically analyzed the context in which my narrative took place, from micro to macro levels. In this case, the micro-level contexts included my personal

Whiteness, maleness, socioeconomic status, my relationship with Kayci, her mother, her councilor, other teachers, our school curriculum, and the rigor present in our classrooms. Macro-level contexts included the systems we operated in, like a two-track educational system, a White supremacist educational system, and a patriarchal educational system. When using a critical lens to examine both the micro and macro context I operated within, I began to ask myself questions such as How did my personal Whiteness, maleness, or power as a teacher show up? Now, it's clear to me that I believed in meritocracy, not a two-track educational system, or the privileges unfairly bestowed by my race, gender, and socioeconomic status. This belief led me to reinforce the ideals of meritocracy with Kayci—erasing both our races, genders, and socioeconomic status in the process. I saw neither myself nor my student clearly.

Reflecting, I strive to see clearer now. Reflecting, I could no longer replicate lies and still bare to look at myself critically, which I need to do to stay authentic. Reflecting, I would need to drastically alter my subject matter and pedagogy to be in the important interest of Kayci, not in the interest of replicating the status quo. As I critically examine myself and the context I exist in from micro to macro levels, I naturally and continuously adapt. If I don't, I am no longer being authentic.

When we neglect to be authentic, we open ourselves up to oppression. Sharon Salzberg (2017) teaches us that neglecting who we are can leave us trapped by expectations of others and potentially dominated by others. But when we embrace our emotions, bodies, and thoughts we begin to hold what we know, want, fear, and feel in a space of self-awareness and self-compassion. It is on this path to self-awareness and compassion that we innately focus on subject matter that is in the interest of learners, for how could we do anything else and still bear to embrace our whole selves simultaneously? How could I teach my students useless and oppressive subject matter and still bear to look at myself honestly in the mirror?

Through this understanding of being an authentic educator, we can find many direct lines to social justice. As Parker Palmer (1998) notes in the opening quote for this chapter, one cannot know their students or their subject, at the deepest levels of embodied, personal meaning, if they do not know themselves. Being authentic allows us to understand and question ourselves, our relationships to students, our curriculum, our power dynamics, hierarchies, systems of oppression, and so much more. Being critical of ourselves, others, our relationships, our environment, and our subject is essential to designing curriculum that I would argue deconstructs intersectional systems of oppression and empowers loving, self-determined scholars oriented toward positive relationships and connectedness.

Being authentic can look like making critical decisions about the content we choose to teach, how we teach it, and evaluating how it personally relates to us and our students—versus teaching concepts that are removed from our being. Building off of a critical analysis of power dynamics naturally leads one to our next principle.

2. Hone Your Intersectional Worldview

Essential Questions: Which of your identities offer you privilege? Which of your identities are marginalized?

Visualize a birdcage. Marilyn Frye (1983), radical feminist theorist and White woman, teaches us that like a birdcage, oppression is a collection or system of intersecting barriers pressing and holding people down. In the metaphor, each wire represents just one aspect of any given -ism, like one aspect of racism or sexism or classism. If we took a micro perspective and spent our entire lives examining just one wire of the birdcage, or examined each wire independent of the others, we may never see that oppression is actually a cage and not a collection of unrelated wires. To understand oppression, we must step back and see it as a system of intersecting barriers caging people in and pressing people down.

An intersectional worldview requires one to step back, and visualize the entire cage, the cumulative power dynamics of intersecting identity markers. Kimberly Crenshaw, an American lawyer, civil rights advocate, a leading scholar of critical race theory, and a Black woman, created the term *intersectionality* to capture the intersecting nature of oppression and to shed light on often invisible constituents within groups that have been oppressed (Crenshaw, 2015). Specifically, she created the term in direct response to a 1976 civil rights lawsuit in which a judge ruled that while Black women could not get a job at General Motors because they could not have a White female secretary job or a Black male factory job, GM was not discriminating in hiring because both Black men and White women could get jobs at GM. The judge ruled one could not combine race and gender discrimination simultaneously.

In response to this ruling, Dr. Crenshaw proclaimed we must take into account the cumulative nature of oppression and privilege—in this case, the judge should have taken into account the cumulative forces of racism and sexism upon Black women trying to get a job at GM. In creating the term, Dr. Crenshaw defined it as a way of thinking about identity and its relationship to power. The term was specifically designed to shed light on often marginalized groups of people within movements who claimed to represent them, for example, people of color, homeless youth in LGBTQI movements, transgender women in feminist movements, or people with disabilities in movements to address police violence. Intersectionality gives many advocates a way to make the often invisible visible, the overlooked included, or the marginalized centered.

Intersectionality is a way of analyzing our world that takes into account all of a person's or groups' identities in relation to power. Building on this idea, intersectionality reveals that in the US, the further one is from the standardized "norm" of a White, Christian, wealthy, heterosexual, able-bodied, cisgender male, the more layers of prejudice the individual in question must face, and the more intersecting wires of oppression that will cage them in. More than analysis, intersectionality is meant to center those who are the most marginalized, most othered from the standardized "norm" in society. Additionally, it should always include an analysis of race, to help ensure, as it was initially intended, that women of color do not continue to be left behind.

Think about your identities: race, sex, sexual identity, gender identity, class, age, ability/disability status, citizenship/immigration status, religious affiliation, etc. Which identities offer you the most privilege? Which identities form your matrix of domination, that is, your oppression cage? Honing our intersectional worldview allows us to better see our own connections to power, privilege, hierarchy, and oppression. To understand intersectionality, we must personalize it, understand how our multitude of identities intersect to impact our life chances.

Constantly working to understand how intersectionality relates to my own privilege is one of the foundational reasons this book opens with an account of my privileged identities: White, financially stable, male with advanced degrees who holds leadership positions in education. Working toward an intersectional worldview is also why I repeat so many times in this book that we all need to center and follow those who have been most marginalized in society toward social justice; we need to follow the lead of women of color. Incorporating an intersectional worldview directly relates to orienting curriculum toward social justice because it allows us to see and center those most marginalized, and it allows us to understand, see, and name the complexities of systems of oppression working to press people down and restrict opportunities that we must deconstruct and find the beauty in our complex identities.

Adding more levels of depth to the discussion, we move on to resisting binaries and borders.

3. Resist Binaries and Borders

Trick Question: Who is with us and who is with them?

In US society, we see a great deal of either/or thinking—in other words, binary thinking. Politicians and journalists frame most topics as a debate. We are constantly divided into "us" and "them" whether discussing the latest trends in academia or our broader political views. Barker et al. (2019) write in *Life Isn't Binary: On Being Both, Beyond, and In-Between*, "To consider life from a non-binary perspective is about shifting our framework away from a rigid either/or perspective, towards both/and possibilities, which embrace paradox and uncertainty."

Nonbinary thinking has roots in understanding sexuality and gender but can also be an approach to understanding other aspects of our identities, our relationships, our bodies, our emotions, and how we think about life, politics, the universe, and everything.

To personalize this, currently in the US, there has been a political push to erect physical barriers on our country's southern border. I do not agree with this. This stands in clear opposition to social justice. In turn, just a few years ago, I erected my own metaphorical borders between Trump supporters and myself. I thought in binaries. I thought, *If you support Trump, you are a bigot and therefore a bad person*, the subtext being that I am then, by default, a good person because I do not support Trump. I turned my polarizing into demonizing when the Trump administration enforced a policy to rip babies from their caregivers at the border: no *human* could support an administration that enforces such a policy.

Barker et al. (2019) go on to describe that framing issues as either/or debates is the first step to most conflicts. The second step involves assuming one side of the debate is right and the other is wrong (another binary), and then picking a side—obviously the "right" side. Continuing toward conflict, we polarize into "us versus them"—where *we* are right and just and good, and they are wrong, unjust, and bad (more binaries). Because *we* are clearly on the right side, we find it easier to justify increasingly unacceptable behavior toward *them*. Both believing in our righteousness and/or haunted by the idea that we might actually be on the bad or wrong side actually make us fight even harder to defend our position and do whatever it takes to win versus lose (another binary).

When I look in the mirror honestly, I do many things that I do not believe are good. I never, I mean *never*, wash my recycling; I even throw my recycling in the trash when the recycling bin gets full because I don't want to take out the full bin. I use my car horn liberally, and I obnoxiously speed around cars I deem to react too slowly. I speak condescendingly and arrogantly to people and hold on to spite for too long for those I have perceived to do me or my loved ones ill. I can hurt those closest to me with words after bottling up my emotions. I can mansplain the hell out of anything. I have time and again supported the soft bigotry of low expectations toward my students. As a teacher and school administrator, I have made countless choices that had the potential to negatively affect students' futures. By all my personal measurements of "good" and "bad" actions, I often embody the bad ones. But when I look in the mirror honestly, with lovingkindness, I do not see a bad person. When I look in the mirror, besides seeing an experienced educated thirty-something-year-old with a Hugh Jackman-esque quality about himself, I see a complex individual with many faults I try to work on when I have the capacity to.

I am not equating my behaviors with ripping children from their parents and throwing them in cages. What I am saying is that as humans we are wired to try to perceive ourselves as good regardless of how moral or immoral our actions might be (another binary). But the truth is we are complex, and when we fail to see others' complexities, we walk an imaginary and dangerous line.

Barker et al. (2019) teach us, "Because the idea that we might be 'truly bad' is intolerable, we often find ourselves blaming others in conflict situations. If we cannot be 'bad' or 'perpetrators,' then someone else needs to be. We also start conflating behaviors with people. Here we're not denying that there are terrible behaviors and acts that people commit, but we're not prepared to turn others into monsters either, even though we admit there can be comfort in othering those who hurt us, since this is often the only way we can let ourselves express appropriate anger towards them."

As a father, I feel a wave of visceral anger and sadness in the base of my stomach, my heart, and my soul when I think about babies torn from their caregivers at the US border and separated by physical barriers for days, weeks, months, or more than a year. I look at my daughters, grind my teeth, and think only monsters can do this. And even writing this I have a hard time actually believing a *person* could do this to babies—they must be monsters, not people. Continuing this logic, I find myself believing that therefore only monsters can support an administration that would do this.

I believe the act of othering and dehumanizing a group of people is the only way humans can be led to commit such atrocities, the only way a human can still see themselves as good while committing horrifying acts. Over the long haul, my dehumanizing of individuals who support such atrocities cannot lead to social justice; my dehumanizing in response by nature leads to more hurt and hate.

Upon writing this section, I had multiple reviewers ask how am I working to personally struggle against my desires to dehumanize those who would support ripping babies away from their caregivers and throwing them in cages. The truth is, at some moments, I am able to see past this binary and at some moments I am not. I am complex. When I force myself to stop and intentionally resist my desire to dehumanize in this instance, I think about family. My brother-in-law, whose mother was a Mexican immigrant in the US in the 1970s, is a vehement supporter of dehumanizing policies by the Trump administration. My wife loves her brother, my brother-in-law loves his nieces, my daughters, and I love my brother-in-law. My brother-in-law is not a monster. He is a human. He is complex, and as a human he can be very hurtful and has caused great harm to his family. While reciting rigid hateful rhetoric, I watch him lose some of his humanity. He also has the capacity to love. He is human, not a monster. As I recall, I too can be very hurtful and have at times caused my family great pain. I am also human, not a monster.

Barker et al. (2019) describe the problem with othering those who commit harm is that we become dogmatic in our beliefs. As we start to see our ways of thinking as incontrovertible truth, we lose sight of the view that multiple realities exist at once. As this happens, our worldview becomes narrower and narrower, making it harder for others and even ourselves to live up to our narrow expectations of what is right. As our binary thinking of right and wrong becomes more rigid, we create unrealistic standards and become increasingly judgmental of both others and ourselves—we cannot make mistakes and therefore cannot be fully human. Our standards become impossible to live up to, and we find it necessary to hide our authentic selves from others to avoid others discovering that our actions are actually *wrong*. As noted earlier, once we fail to accept our authentic selves, we open ourselves up to be oppressed.

In reality, we are all complex individuals with both the propensity for atrocities and the propensity for social justice and love. Humans by nature have biases. We often do both *bad* things and *good* things. Additionally, many of the things we do have the ability to be both bad and good in and of themselves simultaneously. Embodying rigid thinking that I am right and *they* are evil monsters can only lead to more pain and suffering.

However, resisting binaries and borders does not mean we should remain neutral or paralyzed. Resisting the binary that all Trump supporters are monsters does not mean we stay neutral in the face of monstrous atrocities like the separation of babies from their parents coming to this country for hope. We must struggle with all of our being against such harmful and monstrous policies and rhetoric and extend a hand to call in more individuals into the act and pursuit of social justice. We must work to dismantle systems, not dehumanize individuals. Moving beyond binaries aids us in understanding the complexities of our world, which helps us to, "Build Bridges not Borders," as Glenn Singleton (National Summit Courageous Conversations, 2019) professes. As we better understand the complexities of ourselves, our society, and the systems we operate in, we learn that we must take a stance in orienting ourselves and our curriculum toward social justice.

4. Don't Be Neutral; Take a Stance

To be authentic, to hone an intersectional lens, and to move beyond binaries and build bridges, we *must* take a stance. We cannot remain neutral. The Brazilian educator Paulo Freire stresses that educators have a duty of not being neutral. Freire (1985) contends that, "Washing one's hands of the conflict between the powerful and the powerless means to side with the powerful, not to be neutral." Not taking a stance means to perpetuate the status quo, it means to side with domination and oppression. Taking a stance means standing against hierarchy, exploitation, subjugation, domination, and oppression.

bell hooks (2000a) succinctly coined the intersecting systems of domination and oppression in the US *the White supremacist capitalist patriarchy*. In following Indigenous teaching, the prolific scholars Waziyatawin, a Wahpetunwan Dakota woman from the Pezihutazizi Otunwe, and Michael Yellow Bird, a man and citizen of the Mandan, Hidatsa, and Arikara, remind us that the formal and informal behaviors, ideologies, institutions, policies, and economies that maintain the exploitation and subjugation of people around the globe stem from *colonization* and that *decolonization* is the stance that will lead to liberation (Waziyatawin & Michael Yellow Bird, 2005). Aman Sium, self-identified Tigrinya, Indigenous, Eritrean, African, and an anti-colonial resister and Erik Ritskes, a White, Christian, heterosexual male remind us that "decolonization does not fit the demands and expectations of the Western Euroversity—it is alive and vibrant, being theorized and enacted in Indigenous communities around the globe through practices such as storytelling" (Sium & Ritskes, 2013).

To stand in opposition to intersecting forms of domination and colonization, we must work to resist and unlearn systems and beliefs that have been ingrained in us. Tunisian decolonization activist, Albert Memmi, writes that, "In order for the colonizer to be the complete master, it is not enough for him to be so in actual fact, he must also believe in its legitimacy. In order for that legitimacy to be complete, it is not enough for the colonized to be a slave, he must also accept his role" (Waziyatawin & Michael Yellow Bird, 2005). Taking a stand begins with questioning our selves, our beliefs, and moves toward our thinking, feelings, and actions.

As a cisgender White man from a socioeconomically stable family in New York City, the White supremacist capitalist patriarchy was the air I breathed growing up. The air I breathed as an educator. The air I still breathe today. It has infected my lungs, my blood, and my beliefs. As a White man, it is hard to escape the intoxicating and noxious fumes of colonization and the White supremacist capitalist patriarchy in this country. That's why I need to actively work to unlearn all that seems so natural, all that seems neutral, and work to unlearn and take a stance in resisting hierarchy, domination, and oppression.

For example, I need to unlearn false, oppressive ideas such as *objectivity* that rely on the illusion of a neutral perspective. Parker Palmer (1993) contends that a whitewashed, middle-class, male version of "truth" shrouded in the illusion of *objective truth* works to dominate people who have been marginalized. Once an objectivist has "the facts," he no longer needs to listen to others, he no longer needs to seek other points of view. Objective facts are, of course, the facts. Palmer notes once the objectivist has their rigid, binary understanding of truth, all that remains is to bring others into conformity with their vision. hooks (2003) builds on this noting that the goal to bring others into conformity with objective truth is where objectivism turns into control and domination—all of which we must resist.

In *Preparing to Teach Social Studies for Social Justice* (Agarwal-Rangnath et al., 2016), the authors found that veteran teachers teaching social studies for social justice naturally describe their work as resistance, using self-proclaimed adjectives such as, "resister," "warrior," "revolutionary," "renegade," and "outlaw." Take a stance, be a resistor, a warrior, a revolutionary, an outlaw, a decolonizer. Take a stance, accept the risks that come from taking a stance, and find accountability for support as you resist.

5. Find Personal Accountability

Essential Question: What are your biases?

We all hold biases. Dr. Sue (2010), a pioneer in the field of multicultural psychology, a prominent researcher of microaggressions, and Asian man, has found that no person or group of people are immune from inheriting the identity-based biases of their society. We do not live in a world free of biases, and we are not perfect, unbiased beings, nor should we strive to set up such unrealistic expectations for ourselves.

I am not implying that we should embrace our society-instilled identity biases and say, "F*** it. I guess the *objective truth* is I'm just doomed to be a racist, sexist, classist, old White guy here, so be it." We need to constantly work on understanding and minimizing our identity-based biases. Honestly working to understand our authentic selves, hone our intersectional lenses, be critical of our world and worldview, resist binaries, build bridges, and take a stance for social justice all support understanding and minimizing our biases. And none of this work needs to be done alone, nor should it if we want our work to go deeper and sustain.

A key to supporting a deeper understanding of self and actions is to find co-conspirators who we are connected to in the struggle. Co-conspirators can help to see and name our blind spots[14] and help to hold us accountable with love. Additionally, given that there are dominant groups and groups that have been oppressed in this country, accountability also means that those of us occupying positions of power and privilege via our identity markers and roles should be accountable to those who are members of groups that have been oppressed or marginalized.

Accountability work can be done at the micro level by humbly listening to those closest to you, though it is also incredibly important to seek out and listen to collective voices of those who are most marginalized and oppressed. Going deeper, accountability is not merely listening to the collective voices of marginalized groups but centering and following these voices. Seeking out these collective voices does not mean that marginalized groups get a seat at the table, but that those with privileged status follow their direction.

---

[14] Aspects of our personalities that may be clear to others but not to ourselves.

Malkia Devich Cyril, who self-identifies as a Black, working class, queer, butch/genderqueer, woman adds that, "Over many years, I've learned that accountability isn't something anyone can hold another to, it is something we can help each other be, within boundaries that keep us secure" (Brown, 2020). In this sense, within the boundaries of personal safety, accountability is not about punishment, it is about personal and community self-work.

In writing *Justice by Design*, I attempted to listen and center both the individual and collective voices of those who have been marginalized in society, and I asked for and compensated a panel of individuals with a diversity of identity markers to review this work to help keep my centering of the margin from becoming appropriation, as well as assist me in spotting and addressing at least some of my numerous blind spots and biases. Through these forms of accountability, I found myself growing, changing, and adapting with every comment, every conversation, every reading. In many ways, writing *Justice by Design* shaped me more than I shaped it.

Recap and Moving Forward

Our first five values and principles revolve around doing our self-work, reflecting on our beliefs, and reshaping our worldview. These values include:

1. Be Authentic
2. Hone Your Intersectional Worldview

3. Resist Binaries and Borders
4. Don't be Neutral; Take a Stance
5. Find Personal Accountability

By addressing who we are, our beliefs, and worldviews in this manner, we are better situated to design meaningful materials for our students; ask more meaningful questions of our students; and listen and learn from our students. In the next chapter, we focus on values and principles more directly related to facing students.

Chapter 6

Nurture Interdependence

We are what we've got. No one can be left to their fuck ups and the shame that comes with them because ultimately we'll be leaving our-selves behind.

— NGỌC LOAN TRẦN (MCKENZIE, 2016), A SELF-IDENTIFIED VIỆT/MIXED-RACE IMMIGRANT, QUEER AND GENDER WEIRD DISABLED WRITER, STORYTELLER, AND ASPIRING EDUCATOR

Essential Question: What values will directly guide your interactions with students and stakeholders in the classroom?

Narrative: Do You?

"Do you?" These two simple words with the added inflection brought on by a question mark destroyed one of my first coaching relationships. I had recently been promoted as a Special Education Coordinator, responsible for coaching and managing all Special Education staff and services in the building.

One service I set up was a resource organization and study skills course. This course was meant to provide several forms of support. First, it acted as a structured study hall with a huge amount of one-on-one teacher guidance for students who needed additional scaffolding to reach grade-level requirements. Second, it provided time for students who struggled with executive function skills such as organizing materials or agendas—time with an instructor to teach and reinforce these skills. Third, it reduced students' work load because it had to take the place of a general education class period.

In my second year implementing this course, scheduling lined up for Ms. B, a White woman, to instruct a 9th-grade resource class with just four boys who all needed additional support to meet grade-level rigor[15]. They also all needed support in developing executive functioning skills,[16] and all benefited from a reduced course load.

In addition to coordinating Special Education services as part of my role, I conducted bimonthly observations and feedback meetings with all Special Education staff.

My huge error came as I was meeting with Ms. B post-observation of her resource class. The observation hadn't gone well. I knew it wouldn't prior to observing though. I had walked by the class enough times in the previous week to know an observation wouldn't go well. There were only four students in the class, but despite the low numbers, it was not an environment filled with high expectations. It was not an environment where students and their growth appeared to matter.

---

[15] See chapter 9 for a discussion of grade-level rigor.

[16] These include a set of mental skills or processes that include working memory, flexible thinking, self-regulation, and self-control, among others. We use these skills every day to learn, work, and manage daily life.

During my observation, students were supposed to be either focused independently, one-on-one with the teacher, or learning new executive functioning strategies as a class—and nothing close to these expectations was occurring. Instead, students were walking around the room, messing around with each other, and joking that they were not getting anything accomplished that they needed to. Ms. B was merely awkwardly smiling at her students while restating simple expectations like, "Time to get to work, boys."

I knew these students well. And while they all struggled to maintain attention, I knew they could all meet the expectations for the class and greatly benefit from it. I'd worked with each student in countless other classes where they met and exceeded these expectations.

I needed Ms. B to be better for our students. Our students needed her to be better. Luckily, I knew Ms. B had the ability to get there.

However, at the time, I lacked the ability to support her to this end as her coach.

When we met post-observation, there was a clear power differential. It was a clear hierarchical difference that was reinforced by my maleness and her femaleness in our patriarchal society, reinforced by my role as manager, and by the idea that I called the meeting, which dictated the trajectory of the meeting and dominated the conversation.

After presenting what I had observed—students off task—I proceeded to question what Ms. B thought the students were capable of during resource class.

Pretty quickly into my questioning, Ms. B looked at me and stated, "What, do you think I don't believe our students are capable of meeting high expectations?"

I shot back, "Do you?"

These were two simple words with the added inflection brought on by a question mark, and the meeting suddenly shifted beneath my feet. Smiles were replaced by silent tension, support replaced with righteousness, and calling in replaced with calling out.

Ms. B looked at me and replied, "That's not fair." Regardless of whether or not it was accurate, I knew it was not productive. I knew it did not support Ms. B in raising the expectations in her class. And I knew it eroded my ability to coach her into the future.

I never addressed the comment afterward with Ms. B. Less than a year later, she gave up her career as a teacher. Less than a year later, one of her four students also left our school for a more restrictive Special Education setting. But less than four years later, one of her students graduated high school and began his college journey after he personally stated numerous times in the 9th grade that he didn't have a chance of making it through high school.

High expectations for students are just as crucial as high expectations for staff because we all matter, we all deserve to be in a focused community of learning, and we often deserve a chance to be called in when we are in this work together.

Nurture Interdependence

Social interdependence exists when the accomplishments of each individual's goals is affected by the actions of others. Despite a push in Western culture toward independence, we are a deeply interdependent species. Down to our bodies' cells, we can see a beautiful model of reliance in many small parts working together. As educators, we constantly depend on policies, administrators, peers, families, and most importantly on our scholars. We must begin our demonstration of this interdependence by making students matter.

1. Make Students Matter

Take a moment to think about the following questions, adapted from Mattering and Marginality activities and notes from R. Webb (2019) and A. Harp (2020):

- ❖ When was the last time you felt that you mattered at work? What were the cues that told you, you mattered? What was the outcome that reinforced your perception that you mattered?
- ❖ When was the last time you felt you did not matter at work? What were the cues that told you, you did not

matter? What was the outcome that reinforced your perception that you did not matter?

At different points on our journeys, we may find it easier to answer when we mattered or we may find it easier to grasp when we did not matter. Regardless of which might come easier, for the most part, people generally prefer to feel like they mattered at work. I personally prefer to matter at my place of work, and I believe I deserve to matter, just as I deserve love. I also believe *you* deserve to matter at work.

After pondering these questions and statements, take a moment to think about the next set of questions in regard to a student you have or had a particularly hard time connecting with:

- ❖ When was the last time you think your student felt they mattered at school? What cues did you use to make this assumption? When was the last time you asked your student if they personally felt they mattered at school? What was their response?

- ❖ When was the last time you think your student felt they did not matter at school? What cues did you use to make this assumption? When was the last time you asked your student if they personally felt they did not matter at school? What was their response?

If you're unable to ask these questions, what about your lived racial experience prevents you from doing so? If your students are unable to answer, what kind of environment can you co-create with them so that they will?

You deserve to matter at work. *Yes, and* your students deserve to matter in school. In defining mattering, Dr. Bettina Love (2019) writes in *We Want to Do More Than Survive,*

> *Mattering is civics because it is the quest for humanity. I do not mean civics narrowly defined as voting, paying taxes, and knowing how the government works; instead, I am referring to something much deeper: the practice of abolitionist teaching rooted in the internal desire we all have for freedom, joy, restorative justice (restoring humanity, not just rules), and to matter to ourselves, our community, our family, and our country with the profound understanding that we must 'demand the impossible' by refusing injustice and the disposability of dark children. Demanding the impossible means we understand that racism, sexism, homophobia, transphobia, Islamophobia, classism, mass incarceration, and US Immigration and Customs Enforcement (ICE) are protected systems that will not be dismantled because we ask.*

As Dr. Love defines it, making students matter at its deepest level requires a struggle for social justice, because it requires we demand the impossible: end all intersecting forms of oppression. Making your students matter requires this demand, to demonstrate that all human beings matter regardless of identity markers, and because oppressive systems stand to make certain people matter less.

Mattering directly relates to both authenticity and intersectionality. Dr. Love affirms that if we neglect an intersectional worldview, we cannot fully know the richness of our students' identities and humanities. If we view our students through a lens of isolated identities, mattering cannot happen because we cannot see, experience, or support student's full selves. Dr. Love (2019) writes that by working to understand our students through an intersectional worldview, we support their mattering, allowing us to build the cultural wealth of our students and their families while simultaneously creating spaces, "where people matter to each other, fight together in the pursuit of creating a homeplace that represents their hopes and dreams, and resist oppression all while building a new future." The goals of mattering are synonymous with the intentions of social justice to deconstruct cages (oppressive systems) and build nests (a brighter connected future).

In addition to fighting intersectional forms of oppression and creating a homeplace, mattering can also be found in the expectations we hold for students.

2. Be Warm and Demanding

If we love our students and believe they matter, we must demonstrate this by believing in their potential, humanity, brilliance, desires, and power both regardless and because of race, class, gender, sexual identity, religious affiliation, disability status, citizenship status, and any other identity markers. When we believe in our students, we must demand our students meet their high potential with love and caring.

There is a vast body of literature on the liberating power of believing in students' academic potentials and the oppressive power a lack of belief imparts on our students. Dating back to the 1960s, researchers Rosenthal and Jacobsen (1968) demonstrated the clear link between teacher expectations and student performance. Through numerous experiments, they found that priming teachers to have low expectations for a random set of their students (by telling them these students were not capable) led to low academic achievement for those students. However, priming teachers to have high expectations for a random set of students led to high academic achievement for those students. Almost fifty years later, researchers solidified this link. In John Hattie's (Visible Learning, 2020) work measuring 252 influences related to student achievement by doing meta-analyses of meta-analyses, he found: Teacher Estimates of Student Achievement is the third strongest predictor of student achievement—behind number two: Student Self-Reported Grades (which captures a student's belief in themselves), and the strongest variable: Collective Teacher Efficacy (which captures a teacher's belief in their potential to positively affect students). Put another way, the three most powerful predictors of student achievement are students' beliefs in themselves, teachers' beliefs in themselves, and teachers' beliefs in their students.

When teachers lack a belief in themselves and/or their students, we find achievement gaps. Let's look at a particularly pervasive and destructive gap in the US. In *Math Is for White People*, Lisa Delpit (2012) reviews decades of research that demonstrates there are no racially predictive "achievement gaps" at birth (though Black babies consistently outperform White babies in cognitive growth directly after birth); however, in the US, a racially predictive gap favoring White students appears after children enter school. Delpit demonstrates that this gap is due to a lack of belief in Black children. She explains,

> *The problem is that the cultural framework of our country has, almost since its inception, dictated that 'black' is bad and less than and in all arenas 'white' is good and superior. This perspective is so ingrained and so normalized that we all stumble through our days with eyes closed to avoid seeing it. We miss the pain in our children's eyes when they have internalized the societal belief that they are dumb, unmotivated, and dispensable... What happens when we assume that certain children are less than brilliant? Our tendency is to teach less, to teach down, to teach for remediation. Without having any intention of discriminating, we can do harm to children who are viewed within a stereotype of 'less than.'*

The idea of teaching less, down, or for remediation is often referred to as *the soft bigotry of low expectations* that I know I have been culpable of during many of my years teaching (as demonstrated in several of my personal narratives throughout this book). To counter this, we must believe in our students and hold high expectations for them. Lisa Delpit's solution is to become *warm demanders*. Through her exploration, she has found warm demanders support students in realizing that they can achieve beyond anything they may have believed. Delpit defines the first part of being a warm demander is, "academic press," meaning that the academic content students are to learn is rigorous[17]. Students are held accountable for their performance with the content, and students are provided the assistance needed to achieve deep understandings of the content. This is the "demand" aspect of warm demanders.

The second is termed "social support," meaning that there are strong relationships, with deep caring, among students and adults in and out of school. This is the "warm" part of warm demanders. Because warm demanders care deeply for their students, they show real concern about students' not living up to their academic potential. Delpit writes, "The caring, the persistence, the pushing—all these create trust. It is the trust that students place in these strong teachers that allows them to believe in themselves. It is the teachers' strength and commitment that give students the security to risk taking the chance to learn."

In terms of curriculum development, upholding the "demander" side of high expectations means we must start with rigorous, grade-level content[18] and questioning (more on this in chapter 9). Upholding the "warm" side means we are loving and

---

[17] See chapter 9 for a detailed discussion of the term *rigor*.

[18] See chapter 9 for a discussion of what rigorous grade-level content refers to.

authentic, that we strive to develop curriculum that is relevant[19] and facilitates students mattering, along with relationships in a community of learners and risk takers.

3. Build Community

Essential Question: What communities do you find personally rejuvenating and restoring?

When we build community in our classrooms, through our actions and curriculum, we create a space where students matter. As social justice visionaries like bell hooks, Adrienne Maree Brown, and Bettina Love all profess, people oriented toward social justice must inherently build community. Adrienne Maree Brown (2017) documents that an innovative branch of science is finding that species only survive if they learn to be in community. This is because scientists are realizing Natural Selection is not actually individual but mutual—there is no survival of an individual in a vacuum who is fittest, only survival of organisms that adapt to mutually benefit each other in shared environments.

Whether using SEED's metaphor of nest building, the scientific term of mutualism, or taking Dr. Love's (2019) direct words that the road to liberation means creating a, "'beloved community,' a community that strives for economic, housing,

---

[19] See chapter 9 for a discussion of what relevant curriculum refers to.

racial, health, and queer justice and citizenship for all," social justice requires community.

I use the term *community* to describe the feeling of fellowship with others. Being connected through relationships. Relationships are often a key to taking moral action. They allow us to go deeper than surface-level knowledge does. For example, Mark Warren (2010), a self-identified White cisgender male professor, from a blue-collar family and current activist-scholar argues that White folks in particular truly deepen anti-racism activism through relationships with people of color. He writes, "White activists start with a moral impulse that racism is wrong because certain values they care about are being violated. Through relationships, they deepen their commitment as they develop an ethic of caring." Our relationships make the consequences of racially oppressive policies and actions against people of color real and connect us to our true humanity—our authentic, emotional, and moral self. For people who hold privileged identity markers, relationships with people who hold marginalized identity markers allow us to move past surface-level knowledge of oppression toward deeper embodied feelings, more personalized understandings of oppression and moral action.

Taking this same framework broadly in the struggle against all intersecting and oppressive *ism's*, relationships across identity markers can help to deepen our commitments to social justice. In the end, call it community, collaboration, fellowship, relationship, partnership, or mutualism, we need to be connected to one another to end domination, do more than survive, and build our nests united by love.

Despite a general focus in White US narratives to be an independent lone maverick, we are all connected to each other and to this planet. Around the world, many cultures recognize, support, and reinforce our interdependence (Johnson et al, 2008; Zehr, 2014). Yet in the US, K-12 education is often structured around independence. We earn our own independent grades irrelevant of what our peers do, we often make sure to "mind our own business," and I have personally used the phrase "voices off, silent independent work time," in more instances than I could ever count.

The vast majority of our classrooms are structured to support independence, not interdependence (Johnson et al, 2008). To move toward social justice where we see and appreciate the connections between each other and our planet, we must build community in our classrooms and resist putting up borders or dominating and putting folks down.

4. Call Folks In

Essential Question: Again, what are your biases?

As we sharpen our intersectional lenses for social justice, as we better understand the complexities of ourselves and our world, and as we strive to take a stance, there will inevitably be moments when we witness or experience a person who has said something biased or promoted oppression, and there will most likely be moments when our personal biases come out in such ways. For those looking to build a loving community and to counter dominance and oppression, taking action in the face of bias and oppression is key. However, how one addresses such transgressions can have different impacts.

Given the natural fragility of the human ego in our society, calling out often acts to both shame and guilt. Calling in takes a slightly different tactic. While calling in can happen publicly or privately, its key feature is that it's done with love. Instead of shaming or guilting someone who might have made an unintentional mistake, calling in requires one to patiently ask questions to explore what was going on and why an individual might have committed a harmful action. For call-ins to work, there need to be agreements between people who work together to consciously help each other expand their perspectives. Calling in encourages vulnerability to admit mistakes, recognize room for growth, and commit to doing better. Calling in cannot minimize harm already inflicted; however, questioning while calling in can work to get to the root of why the harm occurred in the first place, and it can hopefully stop it from happening again.

I think calling in is particularly important when one holds more privilege and power in a relationship. In my opening narrative, I did not call in my colleague, I shamed her. Calling in is a particularly important tool to use with students—to call our students into our classroom communities in solidarity helps to demonstrate that all students matter. Calling students out can tear them down, while calling in can build them up.

In *We Will Not Cancel Us*, Adriane Maree Brown (2020) asks that we, "look at each other with the eyes of interdependence, such that when someone causes harm, we find the gentle parent inside of us who can use a voice of accountability, while also bringing curiosity—'Why did you cause harm? Do you know? Do you know other options?'" In many ways, she asks that in certain situations we hold ourselves and others in loving accountability: accountability that allows us to pick up those who fall; accountability that uses a parent's voice of discipline, that is warm, demanding, and uplifting; accountability that allows us to move away from punishment and oppression towards hope and transformation.

Discussing calling in, activist Ngọc Loan Trần writes in *The Solidarity Struggle: How People of Color Succeed and Fail at Showing Up For Each Other in the Fight for Freedom* (McKenzie, 2016),

> *I picture 'calling in' as a practice of pulling folks back in who have strayed from us. It means extending to ourselves the reality that we will and do fuck up, we stray and there will always be a chance for us to return. Calling in as a practice of loving each other enough to allow each other to make mistakes; a practice of loving ourselves enough to know that what we're trying to do here is a radical*

> *unlearning of everything we have been configured to believe is normal. And yes, we have been configured to believe it's normal to punish each other and ourselves without a way to reconcile hurt... when we shut each other out we make clubs of people who are right and clubs of people who are wrong as if we are not more complex than that, as if we are all-knowing, as if we are perfect. But in reality, we are just really scared. Scared that we will be next to make a mistake. So we resort to pushing people out to distract ourselves from the inevitability that we will cause someone hurt.*

To reiterate, given that we are not perfect, calling in lets us breathe more easily that others may do the same for us when our biases rear their heads. And while calling in is an important tool, practicing "calling in" should not be in opposition to calling out but rather another strategy existing simultaneously to confront oppressive words and actions, especially when committed by people trying to work together and build community, like teachers and students.[20]

Recap and Moving Forward:

Dr. Bettina Love teaches us to make students matter. Four values and principles we reviewed in this chapter that directly support our work with students include:

1. Make Students Matter

---

[20] Read Brown (2020), *We Will Not Cancel Us*, for an incredibly thoughtful, and supportive piece for recognizing when to call someone in and how to.

2. Be Warm and Demanding
3. Build Community
4. Call Folks In

By creating a community where it is safe to make mistakes because we know we will be called back in when we stray, where we are held to high expectations and demands with love and warmth, and where we struggle together for liberation is to make members in your community matter. While all of the principles and values mentioned so far can be difficult to enact and maintain, it is important to stay grounded and optimistic.

Chapter 7

Stay Grounded

Education is the belief in Possibilities. It is a belief about knowledge systems. It is a belief in the capacities of ordinary humans. We as educators must refuse to believe that anything in human nature and in various situations condemns humans to poverty, dependency, weakness, and ignorance. We must reject the idea that youth are confined to situations of fate, such as being born into a particular class, gender, or race. We must believe that teachers and students can confront and defeat the forces that prevent students from living more fully and more freely. Every school is either a site of reproduction or a site of change. In other words, education can be liberating, or it can domesticate and maintain domination. It can sustain colonization in neo-colonial ways or it can decolonize. Teaching is the unlimited potential of practical problem solving and the transmission of knowledge and values. It is creating a path of practices of learning and innovation, depending on skills and cooperation. Teaching is the psychology of hope, and hope is a cause and a consequence of action.

— MARIE BATTISTE (2017), whose self-identified markers begin with her Indigenous connections and relations, first a member of her Mi'kmaq Nation, and second to the location of those relations with whom she has the deepest connections and with whom she has an established relationship, that is, a registered member of Micmac Aroostook Band and a registered member of Potlotek First Nation. She also references her parents and acknowledges the language they shared with her and from which her Indigenous knowledge derives. She is a mother of three grown children, one of whom is the first

Mi'kmaq to be a member of Parliament in the Canadian government; and she is a grandmother.

Essential Question: What values and principles for social justice will keep you positive, grounded, and healthy in a world ravaged by colonization, hierarchies, and domination?

Narrative: The White Privilege Conference

When I first heard my colleague was attending the White Privilege Conference (WPC), I was like, "You're going where? Is this some kind of Alt Right group? You hanging out with Neo Nazis? What is this about? I thought you opposed racism?"

A few years later, I found myself participating and loving my time at WPC.

WPC is not an Alt Right, Neo Nazi racist conference. WPC was formed twenty-two years ago by Dr. Eddie Moore Jr. at The Privilege Institute, and to this day is one of the only national conferences, created, owned, and operated by Black people. WPC is designed for anyone committed to anti-racist work, which by its nature needs to be intersectional—committed to dismantling White privilege along with all forms of intersecting oppression.

Upon checking in as presenter my first time at WPC, one of the organizers asked me how I was feeling.

"Nervous, excited... I think I feel ready to present? It feels like a lot right now."

"I can understand," she replied. "My friend told me to have fun as I departed for the conference, as if I was going on vacation. I was like, 'It's not really about having fun...,' though I guess in a way it is."

I instantly grasped what she meant. As a White man attending workshops and White affinity caucus groups centered on deconstructing White supremacy, I do a lot of honest looking in the mirror at WPC. A lot of difficult, critical self-work. While there, I've found myself asking:

- So that thing I do is called White fragility[21]? That's embarrassing.
- So that other thing I do is called White control[22]? That's terrible of me.
- So social justice is about both deconstructing cages and building nests,[23] meaning the curriculum I was so proud of that only deals with deconstructing cages is one sided and therefore reinforcing the victimization of marginalized groups? I have a lot of revising to do.
- So all those values such as *grit*, *curiosity*, and *optimism* our charter school was founded on are actually forms of White supremacy and domination in this context?[24] Sh*t,

---

[21] See *White Fragility* by Robin DiAngelo for more information.
[22] See Peggy McIntosh's talks on "White control."
[23] See Jondou Chase Chen's writing quoted in chapter 4.
[24] See *We Want to do More Than Survive* by Bettina Love (2019) for a detailed description of why.

my school principal is not going to like hearing this when I get back.

- ❖ Wait, so White Nationalist groups in the US are way more organized and technologically advanced when it comes to recruiting young White male students than anti-racist groups? We are F*****ed.

I am by no means alone. Each day at WPC ends with the opportunity to participate in small racially segregated affinity groups to process with peers. In my first year at WPC, a female member of my White affinity group broke down in tears after day one, stating over and over how she was not responsible for White privileges, for racism. "It's not my fault," she sobbed. By day three, she looked back at her reaction on day one and chuckled. She stated she could not imagine having that reaction of extreme guilt and White fragility now after her revelations over the three-day conference. That is some serious, difficult, self-development in three days that still brings me joy to recall.

I remember another White male educator in my affinity group stating he came to the conference to bring back more racially equitable teaching strategies to his school but found he wasn't bringing back any. Instead, he realized he needed to spend his time at the conference focusing on his own beliefs and worldviews; he needed to do some serious self-work. He wasn't bringing back teaching strategies, but he was bringing back a teacher better prepared to teach.

My time at WPC is always fun—in a sense. It is liberating. It is empowering. It is where I find myself connected to other White people and other BIPOC in solidarity. It is a place where I find both joy and hope.

I love the space created by Dr. Eddie Moore Jr. and countless others. It is a difficult space, a space where people often have breakdowns and breakthroughs. But it is also a loving space, a space where we learn how to find our inner superheroes for social justice, where we connect with people in the struggle, where we work to call each other in.

Staying Grounded

I often feel overwhelmed in regard to the struggle for social justice, whether in my curriculum writing, my work, or my life more generally.

When I think about the issues facing our educational system, I feel overwhelmed. How can I address the statistic that area code is the best predictor of long-term educational outcomes, or the fact that countless babies are locked up at this moment in cages across our nation, denied the most basic level of safety that schools should be able to provide? How can children feel safe in any school with the dramatic increase and normalization of school shootings over the past two decades? The social reproduction designed into our educational system to support the White supremacist capitalist patriarchy feels like a tidal wave, or more aptly a series of tidal waves, one after the other that has ravaged our country for the past four hundred years, a series of tidal waves that I have ridden to my success.

When I think like this, I feel overwhelmed. How can I push back the rising waters? Not just metaphorically, I mean there are literal rising waters given our climate crisis, and yet in far too many places we have classrooms that still pretend climate crisis is fake news. In far too many places, environmental injustice intersects with class and racial injustice, detrimentally affecting those already marginalized by society[25]. How can I push back the tides? How can I push back the tides while I am riding the waves of White supremacy and patriarchy and capitalism to my benefit? I feel overwhelmed.

When these feelings arise, *emergence* gives me hope. *Emergent Strategy*, as laid out by Adrienne Maree Brown (2017) is a framework to embody social justice. Brown writes: "The crisis is everywhere, massive massive massive. And we are small. But

---

[25] While not given detailed attention in this book, environmental justice is social justice. Climate crises and exposure to environmental hazards (e.g., pollutants, industrial sites, and hazardous waste sites) have disproportionate negative impacts on groups from marginalized communities throughout the world (often disproportionately affecting Black, Brown, and Native communities in the US), increasing the likelihood of health issues and/or learning disabilities, without supplying any of the benefits deriving from the hazards or creation of climate crises that accrue to polluters and many industries.

emergence notices the way small actions and connections create complex systems, patterns that become ecosystems and societies."

As outlined by Brown (2017), emergence refers to how complex systems can arise from numerous simple interactions. *Emergent Strategy* is about intentionally orienting those simple interactions into a strategy or plan for action and liberation. To support those interested in radical social change, Brown lists a number of values and principles as part of the *Emergent Strategy*. Many of Brown's values and principles are echoed throughout this book as they are echoed throughout both the teachings of other visionaries and the natural world.

The first two groupings of values in Part II of this book (chapters 5 and 6) focused on looking at our reflection in the window, as well as through the window toward our students. I see emergence as looking into the future, and that gives me hope, joy, and pleasure.

I included just three of Brown's teachings here, leaving out several because I think that would get in the way of copy infringement, appropriation, and/or colonizing her work. So again, if you have not already, put down this book and pick up *Emergent Strategy* by Adrienne Maree Brown to get started. Below includes my understanding of three values echoed from *Emergent Strategy* that bring me hope when I think about pushing back the tides of the status quo.

1. Connect Your Body and Mind

Have your feelings, beliefs, thoughts, and actions ever been out of alignment? Mine are constantly out of sync. As my body has been primed, I am quicker to fear (heart racing, stomach clenching) a darker-skinned person approaching me down a faintly lit ally than a lighter-skinned person, despite the knowledge (the thinking) that neither a lighter-skinned nor a darker-skinned person is more likely to do me harm. I am quicker to bring my entire body to believe a student can meet my rigorous expectations when that student's way of thinking reflects my own, despite the fact that I *know* there are many ways of thinking, and mine is not the sole route to understanding and brilliance. Connecting our thinking with the feelings and the beliefs coursing through neurotransmitters, hormones, musculature, and even our bones supports us to fully embody our intentions, our *whys*, our beliefs, and our values to wholly support our actions for social justice.

Beyond the hormones and neurotransmitters flowing through our bodies that bring tangible life to our beliefs and feelings, research is elucidating how we all hold some degree of direct or generational trauma from the White supremacist capitalist patriarchy encoded in our DNA. Self-identified healer, author, trauma specialist, and Black man, Resmaa Menakem (2017), teaches us in his book *My Grandmother's Hands* that trauma, so often inflicted to uphold White-body supremacy as he terms it, is held in our bodies, not just our brains. Therefore, we must engage our full bodies to work through our shared pain toward collective healing and social justice.

Connecting our minds and bodies allows us to feel the ground beneath our feet, the pain held in our bones, and the hope in our hearts to stand for social justice and start our collective journeys.

2. Start Small and Iterate

As described by Brown, using the principles of *Emergent Strategy* to lead to social justice and eventually liberation means that an ideal starting place is to start small. One lesson plan, one unit, one class expands and proliferates.

As our own work proliferates from the small, we, along with it, go through new iterations, new forms, new awakenings as we take risks, letting go of our fears of making a mistake. As we let others in to hold us accountable, we grow, our curriculum evolves, and systems change. Adrienne Maree Brown (2017) teaches us that true transformation often happens in iterative cycles, spirals, and explosions. True transformation rarely follows a linear pattern we can track. Brown goes on to note that we should release our feelings of failure, viewing backtracking as a learning experience, constantly asking ourselves: "How do I learn from this?"

We cannot push back the tides alone, and we do not have to push back the tides tomorrow. But we must start somewhere. *Emergent Strategy* reinforces the idea that it is okay to start small and then iterate. We may continue with small steps or explosions or even back steps as we transform ourselves, our classrooms, and or world. Brown (2017) teaches us that, "Small is good, small is all. (The large is a reflection of the small.)" Emergence also teaches us to find positive momentum on our journey.

3. Sing Hope, Discover Joy, Breed Pleasure

Hope. Speaking on the necessity for hope, Paulo Freire (2018) shares, "Whatever the perspective through which we appreciate authentic educational practice—its process implies hope." In *Teaching Community: A Pedagogy of Hope*, hooks (2003) reminds us that over the past few decades, teachers have worked toward new ways of educating to move oppressive systems of domination, imperialism, colonialism, racism, sexism, and classism to create a pedagogy of hope. To live in opposition to oppression and dominance means to *demand the impossible.* Hope allows us to demand and *do* the impossible, as Mary Grey (2001) declares in *The Outrageous Pursuit of Hope: Prophetic Dreams for the Twenty-First Century*: "Hope stretches the limits of what is possible... Living in hope says to us, 'There is a way out,' even from the most dangerous and desperate situations." In stretching past the limits of what is possible, hope allows us to find joy in the struggle.

Joy. Speaking on joy to be found in social justice, Dr. Bettina Love (2019) proclaims "I am talking about joy that originates in resistance, joy that is discovered in making a way out of no way, joy that is uncovered when you know how to love yourself and others, joy that comes from releasing pain, joy that is generated in music and art that puts words and/or images to your life's greatest challenges and pleasures, and joy in teaching from a place of resistance, agitation, purpose, justice, love, and mattering." There is joy to be found in designing curriculum oriented toward social justice, joy in writing curriculum that resists, and joy that can breed pleasure.

Pleasure. Speaking on the pleasure of social justice activism, Adrienne Maree Brown (2019) writes:

> *Pleasure is a feeling of happy satisfaction and enjoyment. Activism consists of efforts to promote, impede, or direct social, political, economic, or environmental reform or stasis with the desire to make improvements in society. Pleasure activism is the work we do to reclaim our whole, happy, and satisfiable selves from the impacts, delusions, and limitations of oppression and/or supremacy. Pleasure activism asserts that we all need and deserve pleasure and that our social structures must reflect this. In this moment, we must prioritize the pleasure of those most impacted by oppression... Pleasure activism includes work and life lived in the realms of satisfaction, joy, and erotic aliveness that bring about social and political change. Ultimately, pleasure activism is us learning to make justice and liberation the most pleasurable experiences we can have on this planet.*

It is imperative that we maintain hope, discover more joy, and make designing and teaching curriculum oriented toward social justice one of the most pleasurable experiences we can have as educators. So if you are not already, start singing hope, discovering joy, and breeding pleasure.

Recap and Moving Forward

Okay, Part II was a bit long. Take a deep breath in... out... You made it—unless you skimmed the titles or just skipped to the recaps, in which case you also made it, but you might not need that deep breath. Side note: Mindful deep breathing is actually great to partake in all the time for any reason, so even if you skimmed or skipped to this point, I invite you to go ahead with that deep breath anyway, focusing your attention and intention on it. Breathe in... out....

Given that Part II is really a collection of summaries, it seems odd trying to summarize it more. Instead, I'll say remember it is important to take time to articulate your own principles and values for orienting curriculum toward social justice. What descriptive action statements stand out to you as your personal guiding values? What principles will you stand on? Maybe take time to write them down right now. Throughout the rest of this book, you will encounter several instances where I take a practice back to the guiding principles and values in Part II. If your principles and values differ, throughout the rest of this book think about how the practices mentioned might align with your personal *how*.

Part III

The What

Chapter 8

Phase Theory

Perfectionism is the voice of the oppressor.

— Anne Lamott (2019), is a renowned author and activist who self-identifies as a White woman.

Essential Question: What does curriculum oriented toward social justice look like?

Narrative: Curriculum Writing

I love teaching. I also love writing curriculum. A curriculum dear to my heart was a set of lessons I designed for half a year of instruction titled: *Introduction to Critical Literacy: Constructing an Intersectional Worldview*.

The curriculum covered an introduction to social justice, race theories, class theories, gender theories, and intersectionality. To accomplish this, it included a collection of rigorous close readings that intertwined grade-level standards with social justice content, meaningful personal application exercises, and creative assignments.

It was initially co-conceived to be used in a 9th-grade human geography class where I co-taught, but it took on many new iterations from there.

The second iteration came when I proposed to my co-teacher that we publish our curriculum. In this second version, we formalized the curriculum, revamped the readings, and reformatted it for easy implementation. It also underwent a review by an accountability panel consisting of members with marginalized identity markers to help us minimize bias in our curriculum.

The third iteration came when I found much of the curriculum did not live up to the ideals of deep understandings for social justice (reviewed in chapter 12). Previous versions were driven more by covering vocabulary, not personally applying skills and content for social justice.

The fourth iteration came when I worked with Guided Pulse to adapt all content for online adult facing learning with podcast-style audio and interactive video content. I pared down the number of questions asked, revised certain readings, and reorganized much of the content.

The fifth and most recent iteration involved a drastic restructuring to incorporate more "nest building"—in all earlier iterations, the curriculum focused more on dismantling oppressive systems instead of also supporting empowerment and connectedness.

Despite five drastic revisions over the years, I view the curriculum as far from complete. I hope to make some important adjustments more relevant to current realities that keep me up at night—and which I am sure will lead to a revised set of course readings, questions, projects, and other materials in the future. Along this path, it will also need more accountability reviews and, ideally, co-creative input.

Here, Gloria Ladson-Billings (2014), the pedagogical theorist and acclaimed teacher educator who self-identifies as a Black woman shares words that give me hope:

> *Scholarship, like culture, is fluid, and the title of this essay, 'Culturally Relevant Pedagogy 2.0: a.k.a. The Remix,' is intended to reflect this fluidity. The notion of a remix means that there was an original version and that there may be more versions to come, taking previously developed ideas and synthesizing them to create new and exciting forms... Such revisions do not imply that the original was deficient; rather, they speak to the changing and evolving needs of dynamic systems. Remixing is vital to innovation in art, science, and pedagogy, and it is crucial that we are willing to remix what we created and/or inherited.*

I already know that even after my sixth and seventh rewrites of any curriculum, it will not have arrived. It will still have years and several revisions and iterations and remixes left to create.

Unit planning is a creative process. Social justice is an activist process, and neither of these processes are simple and linear. And that is okay. Or at least, I tell my obsessive compulsions in the late hours of the night when I can't stop thinking about all the edits and rewrites I would like to make... It is all right... The revisions and remixes will come in time as they are supposed to.

Part III: The What

To reiterate: *This book exists to support educators in using the tenants of backward planning to intentionally create rigorous interdisciplinary curriculum oriented toward social justice and to repair harm that may be caused along the way.* In Part III, we get to *what* specifically this process and outcome might look like.

Note that it took eight chapters to get here. The work we do prior to our actual design work (setting and understanding our intentions, working on our personal beliefs and worldviews being critical of ourselves and the world around us) is important work if we are to design curriculum oriented toward social justice. Social justice is both a process and a goal.

"Prior" might be a misleading word. We should not wait until we have "completed" our self-work before sitting down to work on writing curriculum oriented toward social justice. Our world can't wait for us educators to personally *arrive* before working on more meaningful curriculum for students. Self-work is ongoing, and it should take place *while* and *through* writing and teaching curriculum oriented toward social justice. Educators and students can and should work in tandem while growing and learning. And educators should foster a space where what Christine Saxman calls, "loving accountability" and trust is possible and subsequently present.

Part III of this book is conceived to provide educators with specific tools to design *what* they will present and provide to students. For a first step in understanding *what* we want to present and provide to students, Peggy McIntosh shares a beautiful developmental framework.

Phase Theory:

Peggy McIntosh (1981, 1983), the pioneering White woman feminist and anti-racist activist who helped many of us White people visualize the often invisible (according to what we are taught and subsequently choose not to see) advantages of White privilege in modern times, has written for the last forty years on the topic of developing intersectional curriculum and classrooms. She proposes five phases of development as we work toward creating "wholeness." These phases include:

I. Domination

II. Assimilation

III. Resistance

IV. Inclusion

V. Wholeness

On a continuum of exclusionary to inclusionary, curriculums in Phases I and II can be thought of as being much more exclusionary and Phases III, IV, and V much more inclusionary. As McIntosh originally shared in 1983, to understand each phase, let's think about each in terms of a US history class curriculum. The boundaries between phases are not always discreet but are useful in understanding where we are and what we can work toward.

In a Phase I (Domination), US history curriculum content would only cover the achievements of White men. In Phase II (Assimilation), the content might include a few "token minorities" or White women or women who identify as BIPOC participants in US history, such as Frederick Douglas, Susan B. Anthony, or Sacajawea. In Phase III (Resistance), discrimination or barriers against groups that have been oppressed is the focus. The history of people who identify as BIPOC or as women or non-binary might be included as anomalies in US history or as a people who have been victimized and are powerless. In this view, curriculum assumes there is a normative group and othered groups. While it does shed light on systems of oppression, it can be inherently racist or sexist, for example, covering topics such as enslavement or Jim Crow from a Black-people-as-victims-only perspective versus shedding light on the Black power in resistance and the White role as oppressor during these racially biased atrocities. At its strongest, Phase III (Resistance) is about deconstructing cages but lacks building nests.

In Phase IV (Inclusion), *only* the lives of people of color or women might be the focus of the curriculum in courses like Chicano studies or women's studies. Here, materials tend to be nontraditional. Pedagogies naturally shift away from teacher-centered learning (the teacher is no longer the expert—people are experts in their own identities), and discipline boundaries break down. McIntosh (1983) writes that students in these courses begin to see that, "boundaries between disciplines serve to keep our present political, economic, and social arrangements in place." While Phase IV (Inclusion) curriculums are important and are needed in greater numbers over courses in Phase I, II, and III, McIntosh also notes that in such courses as women's studies there is a danger that they can fall into the same traps as Phase I (Domination), that is, they can cover only the truths of privileged women, failing to take an intersectional view, omitting the truths of women of color or transgender women of color.

In our US history example, McIntosh (1983) describes Phase V (Wholeness) as, "The Lives and Cultures of People of Color Everywhere as History," or "History redefined and Reconstructed to Include us All." Phase V supports students in constructing an intersectional worldview. Phase V must also include the stories of all of us—the ugly/the beautiful, the oppression/the resistance, the exclusion/the inclusion.

As such, Phase V (Wholeness) curriculum cannot be taught in an oppressive manner. As one moves from Phase I (Domination) toward Phase V, pedagogy shifts from a hierarchical or vertical power structure to a flat or horizontal power structure around Phase IV (Inclusion), and then toward a circle encompassing all (vertical and horizontal power structures) in Phase V. Hierarchies, or vertical structures, are inevitable in a classroom setting: though there is a difference between hierarchical roles such as dictator, sage, or guide. Flat or linear relationships are not inevitable, but valuable—as we unlock power in our classes when any stakeholder has the opportunity to act as guide and learner.

Building intersectional curriculum that incorporates both dismantling cages (oppressive systems) and building nests (our interconnected futures) gets us closer to a Phase V curriculum, which gets us closer to wholeness. However, do not plan to develop the model of an all-encompassing curriculum overnight. In her initial 1981 paper describing these phases, Peggy McIntosh shares a story where she asks an expert on how she might go about writing an intersectional textbook titled *American History*. The answer she received was, "I couldn't begin to do that; it is too early. It would take a team of us, fully funded, two years just to get the table of contents organized—just to imagine how we would categorize it..., But don't worry, we were 6,000 years carefully building a patriarchal structure of knowledge, and we've had only twelve years to try to correct it, and twelve years is nothing." While this was over thirty years ago, the perfectly crafted Phase V US history textbook does not exist. We have not arrived. And that is okay, insofar as we continue to make progress and construct new iterations working toward a collective goal.

We will only develop Phase V curriculums through an iterative process whereby we are willing to take risks and start, even as we know our immediate outcomes will not meet the ultimate goals. In light of such daunting work, it can be helpful to view Phase V as a process, more than a destination, because it can only be achieved via a truly inclusive socially just process, as much as social justice itself. Phase V also realizes that once developed, it will be forever evolving class after class because each student who walks through the door will shape the curriculum.

The creative process thrives on remixing. Activism and social justice work as an emergent process thrives on remixing. *Justice by Design*, or designing curriculum oriented toward social justice, is both a creative process and activist process and is therefore iterative by nature. I have found my own path to developing curriculum that leads to deep understanding of social justice issues to be spiraling in nature, frequently following patterns that phase theory can help me better understand, which in turn helps me to better understand phase theory.

Personally Applying Phase Theory

Jondue Chen (2013), co-director of SEED writes, "When I use Phase Theory in my SEED work, I always couch it in the context of my own stories. I have to. We all do. Learning never happens in a vacuum. My research as a developmental psychologist seeks to show in as many ways as possible: context matters. Thus when I explain Phase Theory I use my own stories and then I ask for my participants to think of their own stories to test whether Phase Theory might be useful to them." Applying phase theory to my personal experience provides a useful lens that helps me both better understand phase theory and my own experiences and actions.

Phase I (Domination). Throughout my years in education from student, to teacher, to coach, to administrator, to program manager, I have constantly climbed the ladder, despite my errors, my various spelling and grammar mistakes, and my missteps, and the system supported my ascension virtually unscathed. And as I climb higher, I have continued to receive more money, praise, power, and influence. Time and again I also wield the influence that my work identity imparts to give credence to my ideas and goals. My career experiences to this day directly resemble a hierarchical mountain or pyramid as laid out by Peggy McIntosh, where the higher on the pyramid I climb the fewer people there, are and of the few people remaining, more and more resemble my racial and class identity markers. I often feel trapped in Phase I in my career.

In the context of my classrooms, when I began teaching Special Education courses in reading and math. my content was exclusive and as far from interdisciplinary as possible, and my pedagogy was all top down. In my early years, I always used the "gold standard" of intervention curriculums in Special Education, which were targeted in subject matter, only reflective of the dominant master narratives and frequently incorporated scripted direct instruction. Take for example a targeted drill and practice algebra curriculum that had no room for interdisciplinary learning or allowing students the opportunity to be anything other than passive receptacles of information and algebra skill building through constantly practicing discrete algebra skills in numerical problem sets out of a real-world context.

Phase II (Assimilation). I clearly remember in 2nd grade doing a project on Frederick Douglass for Black History Month. It stands out because it was one of the few opportunities I had to learn about people in history who were not White. In my private lower school in Manhattan in the 1980s, Black History was different or *other* from our "normal" history and only relegated to one month in the school year. Black history was tokenized, as much as LatinX and women's history were. Native American and Indigenous history was all but erased unless one includes the images of either "peaceful or savage Indians" dealing with the likes of "great White men" like Christopher Columbus or President Andrew Jackson.

As a teacher, in my early years while I shied away from lies like the heroism of Christopher Columbus, I still replicated the tokenization of people who did not fit the image of the White male form: whether it was teaching about a *special* Black male modern artist in my art history course, a *special* White female photographer in my photography class, or interspersing a few key reading excerpts from Langston Hughes or Maya Angelou in my reading classes. I have spent much of my time in front of students tokenizing experiences of women and BIPOC.

Phase III (Resistance). When I first started working in a charter school, I fell into the mental traps of us versus them—them being district schools, private schools, and even *other* charter schools. I thought we had to do things differently: we had to resist the reproductive natures of those other schools because we were different, we were special. And we did do some things differently, sometimes a better kind of *differently* and sometimes not. When we did things differently, I knew we were right and *they* were wrong (even when our practices caused harm). And I so badly wanted to dominate *them* with our egalitarian ways. I was stuck in dogmatic binaries.

At the same time, I also began to develop curriculum specifically for the purposes of both social justice and increasing critical literacy skills. In my first iterations of such curriculums (discussed in the opening Narrative of this chapter), all of my readings and assignments were about resistance, about cage crushing. But the curriculum also had the adverse effect of reinforcing the victimization of those othered, rather than highlighting the power to be found in communities that have been oppressed throughout US history. It was not until attending workshops by SEED and Peggy McIntosh that I began to peek out past a resistance-only mindset. However, I still taught my classes as if I were the expert. I studied the systems of oppression at play that we discussed on a daily basis and class centered my knowledge not others—only I could answer the toughest questions in the room. While I used cooperative learning groups, the class still revolved around me, my expertise, my knowledge, and my dictation.

Phase IV (Inclusion). As I coach teachers or facilitate graduate-level classes, I find myself listening more and taking notes as I learn from those around me. In my curriculum writing, while listening and learning about phase theory, cages and nests, Afrofuturism[26] and Abolitionist Teaching[27], and decolonizing methodologies[28], I began to see my curriculum as interdisciplinary—incorporating critical literacy with close readings, talking Circles[29], creative writing, visual arts, statistics, and empowerment. Again, I do not believe I have arrived. I still have a long road of self-discoveries to make. But I am working on it, working on better understanding the context in which I personally live and on better seeing myself in the mirror.

---

[26] Afrofuturism is a cultural aesthetic, philosophy of science and philosophy of history that explores the developing intersection of African diaspora culture with technology often challenging people to imagine a greater world than the one that currently exists. It was first coined by Mark Dery in his 1993 essay titled "Black to the Future."
[27] See *We want to do more than survive: abolitionist teaching and the pursuit of educational freedom* by Bettina Love for a comprehensive overview of the term.
[28] See *Decolonizing Methodologies: Research and Indigenous Peoples* by Linda Tuhiwai Smith.
[29] See Chapter 9 for a definition and review of *talking Circles*

Phase V (Wholeness): Has my teaching or curriculum entered Phase V? I would say no. But I also don't know that it matters much that we judge where we are using phases, since we are constantly changing and moving just as the world around us changes and moves. In trying to understand Phase V, I think it is about feeling whole, not feeling judged.

There are moments when I am sitting with my family and I feel whole—as my two-year-old makes farting noises to make my six-month-old giggle nonstop, a laughter that infects both my wife and me. There are moments when I finish writing a chapter, or a lesson plan—where every piece seems to click and I feel whole—even if not done collaboratively. And I know there are many more such moments yet to come.

There are also moments when I do not feel whole. When I feel alone. I feel like an oppressor or an imposter or a failure. I do not believe phase theory was created to provide discrete categories meant to judge how good a teacher we are or not, or to judge how woke our curriculum is or not. I think understanding phase theory is about finding hope. A starting place. A destination and a process for progress.

Progress

Ideally, progress leading toward Phase V (Wholeness) can have meaningful impacts. Peggy McIntosh (1983) shares that, "A Phase V curriculum would help us to produce students who can see patterns of life in terms of systems of race, culture, caste, class, gender, religion, national origin, geographical location, and other influences on life which we haven't begun to name. At the same time, Phase V curriculum promises to produce students who can carry with them into public life the values of the private sphere, because inclusive learning allows them to value lateral functions rather than discredit them in the context of paid or public life." In Phase V, one understands power structures; one understands oppressive systems; and in many ways, one begins to understand intersectionality.

In all likelihood, you will not achieve a final draft of your unit plan using the tenets of *Justice by Design* the first time you write it. In fact, you may never achieve a final draft. You may never arrive. But you may find wholeness, and you may even support your students in finding wholeness.

I find personal solace in knowing that classism and patriarchy have existed for 12,000 years (since the Neolithic revolution) and racism and White supremacy for four hundred years (since antimiscegenation laws in Colonial America). But for modern humans, we have existed for at least 200,000 years, far longer than these systems of oppression. For 99 percent of our species' existence, we lacked the structures of dominance we see today (Peter, 2017). We are not oppressive by nature; we have learned these behaviors, and we have time to unlearn them. We have time to get this right. Time to find our whole selves in our curriculum and allow students to find themselves. In the act of working toward a more meaningful, more intersectional, more socially just curriculum, I personally find my whole self. My medicine. My meaning.

Recap and Moving Forward

Phase theory helps us to understand our experiences and actions, to revise our vision for curriculum oriented toward social justice, to understand the collaborative path needed to realize our vision and provide us with *the what* to create: curriculum that is truly inclusive, interdisciplinary, intersectional, and whole.

To achieve this, curriculum must also be rigorous. In the next chapter, we define what rigor can mean before diving into what specific pedagogies oriented toward social justice can look like.

Chapter 9

Rigor and Standards

We need mass-based political movements calling citizens of this nation to uphold democracy and the rights of everyone to be educated, and to work on behalf of ending domination in all its forms—to work for justice, changing our educational system so that schooling is not the site where students are indoctrinated to support imperialist white-supremacist capitalist patriarchy or any ideology, but rather where they learn to open their minds, to engage in rigorous study and to think critically.

— BELL HOOKS (2003)

Essential Question: How do we know we are engaging students in rigorous study?

Narrative: Coaching Teachers

I thought I understood academic rigor, and then I started coaching teachers, only to realize that I had no idea how to set the bar in my own classroom for all my years teaching. My first awakening to rigor came when I observed a 9th-grade writing teacher spending most of a lesson reteaching how to use apostrophes. Walking around the room and reading students' work, I estimated most writing met middle school standards—not 9th grade. And that made sense when a sixty-minute lesson was focused on reteaching how to use apostrophes—a skill far removed from deeper high school core writing goals.

Rather than move to judgment toward this teacher, I stepped back and looked in the mirror. This was one of the first moments where I walked into a room and measured the content being covered, and the work students were producing using grade-level standards. During this observation, I was part of a group of educators in training to be academic coaches—and holding content and student work up to grade-level standards was part of our training. It was a moment that made me cringe, feeling inadequacy and guilt, verging on an imposter complex. How many lessons had I taught in my life? How many of those lessons really aligned to grade-level standards? How often did my students' work truly reach grade-level rigor? How much of my teaching was complicit with the soft bigotry of low expectations[30]?

I *was* that writing teacher for years. Not in writing *per se* (I read way too slowly to give students who are sharing a wealth of brilliance on paper feedback in a timely manner to be a good writing teacher), but I was that teacher in my own domains. And it took me learning how to coach other teachers to turn the mirror on my own practices and to see where I was perpetuating the myth of opportunity, where I could directly say, "Here is evidence that I am reinforcing a two-track system." So, I changed my perspective.

---

[30] The idea of teaching less, down, or for remediation is often referred to as *the soft bigotry of low expectations*. (Bush, 2006)

I changed how I defined academic rigor and how I used grade-level standards to avoid the socially reproductive nature of our educational system.

I began to look at all content, whether it was content I was teaching or content I was observing being taught through a standards-based rigor lens. And more than just content, I focused on student work: writing, speaking, collaborating. I used this new lens to help me gauge: Are students learning, as hooks states, "to open their minds, to engage in rigorous study and to think critically"?

Why Is Rigor Important?

In the US, regardless of race, class, or gender, regardless of living in rural, suburban, or urban communities in the north, south, east, or west, or regardless of going to a district, charter, or private school—K-12, students want to go to college. Students see college as the stepping-stone to desired futures. And that makes sense. According to the US Department of Education (Fact Sheet, 2015) college *is* the stepping-stone to drastically increasing lifetime earning potential, employability, and even life expectancy. It also makes sense that given student aspirations, across all the demographics mentioned above, students are consistently doing what's asked of them in class. The catch is that even though students want to go to college, and are doing what's asked of them in class, our classrooms are not adequately preparing students for their aspirations despite constant assertions from well-intentioned educators like myself that we are. Enter *The Opportunity Myth*.

In a recent nationwide study entitled The Opportunity Myth by TNTP (2018), researchers observed 1,000 lessons, reviewed 5,000 assignments, analyzed 20,000 student work samples, and collected nearly 30,000 hours of real-time student surveys from five diverse school systems (Rural, Suburban, Urban; Charter & District; throughout the US)—it was a comprehensive study. They found that across all the demographics, 94 percent of students want to go to college, 71 percent want careers that require college, students were on task in class 88 percent of the time, and they met the demands of assignments 71 percent of the time. Additionally, when given grade-level assignments, regardless of race, class or gender, students met grade-level demands over 60 percent of the time. However, on average, students had access to grade-level assignments just 24 percent of the time—a statistic that gets better for White students and worse for students of color. Thirty-eight percent of classrooms serving predominantly students of color *never* had access to grade-level assignments, compared with 12 percent of classrooms serving predominantly White students.

Again, according to The Opportunity Myth the vast majority of K-12 students want to go to college and are meeting the expectations put before them in an effort to do so, but our classroom expectations are not meeting students' aspirations. This is especially true for students of color, despite the fact that all students can meet higher expectations. This instructional data matches the outcome data as well.

On one end of the outcomes lies the number of students having to take remedial classes in college, which is estimated to total $1.5 billion annually (ERN, 2016). On the other end, lies the School to Prison Pipeline leading to over 2.3 million people incarcerated with lost opportunities, and a direct annual cost of significantly more than $80 billion (Lewis & Lockwood, 2019). Both these outcomes disproportionately impact people of color and students from lower socioeconomic backgrounds more negatively than wealthy White people.

Meritocracy in the US is an illusion, an imagination that clouds reality. Working hard in classrooms that are not rigorous leads to The Opportunity Myth that we see across this nation. The myth of meritocracy. The fact that we are peddling false promises and wasted time while reproducing a two-track system. From an economic perspective, low rigor costs our country billions. From a social justice perspective, low rigor maintains the status quo and an unequal distribution of resources and opportunities. By naming these realities, we can begin to see through the illusions.

If instruction is not rigorous, it is not supporting opportunities. If instruction is not rigorous, it is upholding inequity and a two-track system. If instruction is not rigorous, it cannot lead toward social justice.

So What Is Rigor?

There is a myriad of definitions for the two-syllable, five-letter word *rigor* that goes on for pages depending on discipline. Definitions cover *severity, austerity, strictness,* and even *rigor mortis*. I personally lean on the definition that rigor is, "the quality of being extremely thorough, exhaustive, or demanding" echoed in many dictionaries.

In an educational context, while there is not full consensus on a definition for academic rigor, many researchers accept the definition that rigor in academics includes intentionally crafted and sequenced learning activities with opportunities for students to create, demonstrate, or support with evidence their own understanding or interpretation of information (Schwegler, 2019). Using this definition, the depth of rigor can include a wide range of educational practices and content. While the term *rigor* can be taken broadly, I believe it is helpful to maintain a replicable working definition for *rigorous curriculum* that stays away from the whole *rigor-mortis* end of things.

I have found the most useful, valid, reliable, and easy-to-use definition for rigorous curriculum to be curricula that includes relevant questions, tasks, and materials that meet the depth of grade-level standards while providing meaningful opportunities for students to practice grade-level skills. It might be easier to look at this definition in terms of three guiding questions:

1. Do content and questions in the curriculum align to grade-level standards?

2. Do tasks in the curriculum provide meaningful practice opportunities for students.

3. Is the content in the curriculum relevant to students?

A curriculum needs to be able to answer yes to each of the above questions to be considered rigorous. This definition pulls in aspects from the criteria used in TNTPs study, The Opportunity Myth, to measure if instructional tasks met rigorous college readiness standards (which was a new iteration of the EQUIP Protocol from Achieve.org). I do not share this definition to imply that it is perfect. I imagine in ten years I will use a drastically different definition, which may evolve from this one—as such iterations demonstrate progress, and I personally plan to make progress over the next ten years. But for now, I find this definition very useful. A key to finding utility in this definition lies in the words "relevant," and "grade-level standards."

Relevant. Willard Daggett (2009), a male educational consultant writes, "Relevance refers to learning in which students apply core knowledge, concepts, or skills, to solve real-world problems. Relevant learning is interdisciplinary and contextual. It is created, for example, through authentic problems or tasks, simulations, service learning, connecting concepts to current issues and teaching others." In this sense, relevance is about application, about transferring knowledge into real-world scenarios, which aligns well with social justice, as we have a whole lot of socially unjust problems to work on.

Vagle and Reeves (2015) build on this definition in *Design in 5*, as the authors state, "Relevance involves application of concepts in different ways and situations. It is about generating wonder and interest in what we are asking students to learn." When we start to think about words such as *wonder* and *interest* we need to work with students and communities and sharpen our intersectional lens to learn what *wonder* and *interest* mean to our students in the context of our society.

Orienting relevance toward the context of an oppressive two-track educational system—relevance must also include critical thinking[31]. By this, I mean that if we are to form "mass-based political movements calling citizens of this nation to uphold democracy and the rights of everyone to be educated, and to work on behalf of ending domination in all its forms—to work for justice," as stated by hooks, then it is incredibly *relevant* for scholars to learn how to be critical of systems, institutions, practices, rhetoric, and self.

Standards. In any conversation about *thorough, exhaustive, and demanding* academic expectations, we need to talk about standards. Standards aid us in setting a rigorous grade-level bar. Ideally, that is not a racist bar, a classist bar, a sexist bar, or

---

[31] See pages 72 & 164–167 for more discussions around the term *critical*.

otherwise overly biased bar. But what do I even mean by *standards*?

In education, when one uses the term standards, one is usually referring to Math and English Language Common Core State Standards (CCSS)—and these are definitely first in my mind, but so are the Next-Generation Science Standards, the AP History standards, the National Core Arts standards, The National Curriculum Standards for Social Studies, and other various state-specific standards. Basically, all the standards out there, the ones you've heard presidents, politicians, CEOs, and educators praise, are the same ones that you've heard presidents, politicians, CEOs, and educators scorn.

There is a lot of rhetoric around how common core standards in particular were supposed to be the great equalizer—finally realizing the American dream of meritocracy. There is also a lot of rhetoric around how common core standards are destroying education in America. As with most binaries, there are issues with both of these either/or stances.

We *should* question the CCSS given that their formation was largely funded by the Gates Foundation and other philanthropic entities. They were primarily created by business leaders and politicians with little input from educators. After being created ostensibly by corporate America, they were then enthusiastically embraced by the Obama administration with little field testing. Today, following the money, the common core standards movement has financially benefited large-scale corporate curriculum and standardized test writers, leading many to critically question their development and implementation. (Agarwal-Rangnath et al, 2016)

However, moving beyond the context of the CCSS development and who the standards financially benefit, on their own, standards (Common Core or otherwise) are not the great equalizer nor the destroyer of worlds. They do not tell us what to teach, as many fear or rely on them to do. They are not specifically a test, as they are often conflated with. They are not a standardized curriculum churning out robots, as they have been accused of doing. Yes, there are poorly written standards out there that are too big or too specific or too biased. Yes, people have used standards to create and push for more high-stakes testing to the detriment of many classroom environments. But the most widely used CCSS do generally well at reducing bias and providing just the right amount of information to tell us where to set the bar without being overly specific or vague or a high stakes assessment in and of themselves. According to a report by the State of Washington (OSPI, 2011),

> *There is strong agreement within the committee that access to rigorous standards for all students is a critical success factor and the foundation from which the standards can be implemented. The standards define what is essential for successful performance and encourage people to strive for the best. From an equity perspective, by setting high standards for all students, we show that we believe that the quality of*

education offered to 'the best and the brightest' should be the quality of education available to all. Overall, the committee agreed that it is plausible that bias is not in the standards themselves, but within the delivery of instruction and in varied instructional environments.

To underscore this, remember back to the Opportunity Myth—classrooms need to be better at delivering content at a grade level bar. Thirty-eight percent of classrooms serving predominantly students of color and 12 percent of classrooms serving predominantly White students in US K-12 classrooms never have access to grade-level rigor.

So how can standards set the bar? There are a lot of metaphors out there. Wiggins and McTighe (2012) provide a particularly useful one as they parallel standards to building code. They write, "The standards are like the building code... The house to be built or renovated is designed to meet the needs of the client in a functional and pleasing manner—while also meeting the building code along the way." This is a very useful metaphor because it underscores that we should design a curriculum that meets the needs of our classroom while also meeting the requirements of standards. To propose a slightly different take, I personally like the idea of a measuring tape metaphor for standards because this parallels standards to a tool, ready to carry out a very particular purpose in *Justice by Design*.

Just as I pull out a measuring tape to figure out the height and width of my window so I have a better idea of where I want to set my window curtain bar and of what size curtains to use to cover the window, I use standards to figure out what decoding skills I need to cover in 1st grade, which math skills and in what order I should teach them in 7th grade, or what reading skills I should focus on in my 10th-grade literature class. The tape measure does not decide exactly where I set my curtain bar, what material my curtains will be, what color they will be, how far beyond the window I plan to extend them, if the bar will be flush mounted or not, or if I will have motorized curtains connected to Alexa or Siri or Google (I could go on...I know far too much about curtains, but the point of the metaphor remains). The curtain is our instruction, and generally, standards do not tell us *what* to teach, *when* to teach, *how* to teach, or what *colors* or *narratives* to teach. In other words, standards really do not tell us much, and that is a good thing. The tape measure is a tool that gives us basic information needed so that the curtains we design actually meet our goal of covering the window. Standards, the well-written ones, give us basic information needed so that we can design curriculum to meet our shared goal of preparing students for the opportunities they want and deserve, preparing students to be critical thinkers, preparing students to be change agents and pleasure activists[32].

---

[32] See *Pleasure Activist: The Politics of Feeling Good* by Adrienne Maree Brown (2019).

Similar to a carpenter who's been in the field for twenty years and may be able to estimate a foot measurement by eye, there are many skilled teachers who know what rigor looks like without the aid of a standard. But just as there is security in the veteran carpenter using their tape measure, there should be security in the veteran teacher using standards to ensure their work and their students' work meet the bar of rigorous study to open the minds of scholars to think critically and to uphold democracy for all.

Standards tell us where to set a rigorous grade-level bar, and that is it. Standards have been conflated with standardized tests, and here is where I deviate. I think standards are better used as a tool to aid teachers in setting a bar, than used to reinforce high stakes, multiple-choice testing. I also do not pretend to think standards are perfect as a tool. I imagine in the coming years that our national standards in all subject areas are going to be revised using a more inclusive process than was used originally, and standards will go through new iterations and become much stronger and have more user-friendly tools better suited for working toward social justice.

Now that we have reviewed how one-dimensional today's standards are as a tool, we must take the next step of understanding the depth that is often written into that one dimension. Just as we need to understand the lines written onto a tape measure or why the tip of the tape measure moves (spoiler alert: the tip of the tape measure moves by the width of the hook itself depending upon whether you are taking an outside or inside measurement), we need to understand the detail making up the standards in order to use them effectively. Missing just one detail can lead to missing the bar. In other words, if we only cover 75 percent of a standard, we have not actually met the depth of the standard.

To use our tape measure metaphor again, if we measure the width of our window as 25¾ inches, and we fail to notice the ¾-inch detail on our tape measure, we may cut our curtains to 25 inches, and they will fail to cover the width of the window. In terms of content, if the standard is Common Core Reading Literature 5.3 (CCSS RL5.3): "Compare and contrast two or more characters, settings, or events in a story or drama, drawing on specific details in the text (e.g., how characters interact)," the student ask must include comparing characters or setting or events based on specific details to meet the standard and grade-level rigor. But thankfully, because of how one-dimensional standards are, we do not need to stop there.

We can also reach the depth of a standard like CCSS RL5.3 by asking: Compare and contrast privileged and marginalized characters in the text providing details to support your comparisons; then state how these portrayals might illustrate the author's beliefs, or how these portrayals relate to our current society's stratification of privileged and marginalized individuals. In this example, we begin using a critical literacy pedagogy (as discussed in the next chapter) that goes way beyond the basic who, what, where, when, and why formatting of questions suggested by common core, while requiring students meet the grade-level bar on their path toward critical examination (Papola, 2013). By intertwining standards with social justice pedagogies, we can make content more *relevant* to students and social justice, thereby increasing its rigor using our working definition above.

Side note: If new to the world of standards, I recommend that you read the Common Core appendices to understand that standards should never be taught as isolated skills but intertwined in the context of your content.

Recap and Moving Forward

We can define rigorous curriculum as curricula that includes relevant questions, tasks, and materials, which meet the depth of grade-level standards while providing meaningful opportunities for students to practice grade-level skills. While standards are not a perfect tool, they can support us in deciding what content, skills, and tasks are grade-level appropriate. Standards help us know where to place the rigor bar. They contain information we need in order to design curriculum that gives our students access to reach the depth of understanding needed to make opportunities a reality and not a myth—dismantling our two-track system. In the next chapter, we discuss a range of pedagogies that when intertwined with high expectations, like the expectations set by grade-level standards, our other principles and values from chapter 5 can aid in orienting a classroom toward social justice.

Chapter 10

Pedagogies Oriented Toward Social Justice

To even begin to attack our destructive and punitive educational system, pedagogies that promote social justice must have teeth. They must move beyond feel-good language and gimmicks to help educators understand and recognize America and its schools as spaces of Whiteness, White rage, and White supremacy, all of which function to terrorize students of color.

— BETTINA LOVE (2019)

Essential Question: What pedagogies do you gravitate toward, and how can they intertwine with social justice?

Narrative: My First Talking Circle

The first talking Circle I co-facilitated may have caused more harm than it facilitated justice. I was in my fourth year of teaching as a Special Education teacher at the public arts magnet school with a central racial equity mission. At the time I was co-teaching in an 11th-grade statistics class. My co-teacher was another young White man, also in his early years of teaching. I felt it hard to connect with him in part because I was born and raised in NYC, and he came from a very rural and White background—each of our circumstances leading to different kinds of biased White liberal worldviews.

We had both just attended our first training on restorative justice[33] and talking Circles, and like so many teachers after an engaging workshop, neither of us could wait to try out this new pedagogy and extend our instructional practices. During the same afternoon as our training, I sat down with my co-teacher to plan how we could incorporate Circles.

I proposed we introduce Circles into our statistics course by holding a Circle discussion every Friday that revolved around a statistical graph relating to a social justice topic. For me, I felt like it could finally be my first step into creating a classroom-oriented approach toward social justice, despite having little context as to what social justice or even *good* instruction might mean.

Similarly inspired, my co-teacher jumped on board, and we began designing our first Circle lesson to use the following Friday. We decided our first graph would involve statistics relating to the mass incarceration of Black and Brown people in the US. We then structured several rounds of questions for students relating to the data in our proposed graph. To give context, Michelle Alexander's foundational text *The New Jim Crow* had just been published, but there was very little in the mainstream media on mass incarceration and government-sanctioned, racially biased police violence (a topic much more prevalent in the media today in large

---

[33] An approach to discipline that replaces punishment with restoring humanity, building community, and repairing harm.

part due to work by Dr. Alexander and powerful movements like Black Lives Matter).

Our lesson plan began by projecting a graph that clearly depicted the discrepancy in incarceration rates between White and Asian peoples as compared to Black, Brown, and Native peoples. We then planned several rounds of questions, ranging from "What do you see?" growing toward "Why do you think this is?" to "What implications does this have for us?" We had a talking piece that went around the Circle, allowing just one person to talk at a time, following a designated order and giving everyone's voice equal footing. My co-teacher sat across from me in the Circle and started each round.

In general, most of our students identified as Black and Brown, there were an equal number of male and female students, and there were a handful of students with learning disabilities in math, generally students on my caseload as the Special Education teacher in the room.

It's been a long while now, and years of trying to forget this lesson, but I can still remember the gist of what my co-teacher shared as he stated, "So why do you think these disparities exist? I think a lot of it is about a lack of family structure in many Black and Brown communities..." He went on for a few minutes blaming people of color for the disparities in incarceration rates with no mention of systemic, generational oppression, and racist government policies. I sat silently, shaking in my seat, clenching my teeth and chair, and my heart beating fast because I could not believe the door I had opened by pushing my co-teacher to do this particular lesson without reviewing the content with him prior, without taking the time to get to know him or his worldviews in the first place.

So, I had a dilemma. I could let this authority in the room continue his explanation, continue to blame people of color for racial disparities in mass incarceration—unchallenged, to just sit and wait in discomfort until the talking piece went halfway around the Circle and got to me—or interrupt the process, take over the conversation, and steer it in a more socially just direction immediately. It was a hard choice for me at the time.

I decided to wait...heart pounding in my ears, eyes bulging, body shaking, fearing the harm being done...

In retrospect, there are so many changes I would have made in preparing for this lesson. I would have used graphs and data that highlighted proportional rates of drug abuse by race, but dramatically disproportionate rates of drug arrests by race. I would have used different guiding questions growing toward how statistics can be used to support oppressive systems such as mass incarceration and how we can use statistics to dismantle oppressive systems like mass incarceration. I would have reviewed the content and realities of the prison industrial complex and the school and prison nexus[34] with my co-teacher prior to the lesson. I would have built a relationship with my co-teacher, where I better understood his worldview. I would have nurtured trust between us to push his thinking toward a more intersectional worldview. However, given the predicament I was in, given that I did *not* prepare for the lesson as I should have, given that I did *not* even know what I did not know back then, I believe I made the right choice.

After my co-teacher finished his explanation, the next few students agreed with him, reasserting the blame game, and then one brave soul, Nadia, a Black female student, refuted the teacher's assertion, blaming racist policing practices for mass incarceration. Several more students echoed Nadia's sentiments, and James, a Black male student, flatly looked at my co-teacher and told him he was completely wrong. By the time the talking piece got to me, I was following our students' wave of assertions rather than the other way around. Once the talking piece was in my hand, I babbled on about, "I disagree strongly with Mr. S... Generational systems of oppression... Capitalism... White Supremacy...The war on drugs...The New Jim Crow..." Actually, I have no recollection of what I said, but I remember how I felt after the fact. My answer was not important. Or, at least, it was less

---

[34] This term reveals the reality that our schools and prisons represent a single system—inextricably connected, functioning as it was designed to function, rather than a pipeline connecting two independent systems.

important than my student's answers—in particular, James's response.

James had been on my Special Education caseload since the 9th grade. We had an up-and-down relationship. I recall his mother telling me early on in our relationship that he struggles with men, especially White men. By the time he was in my 11th-grade statistics class, he struggled with me. Admittedly, I had let him down on many occasions, spending more time trying to control him than work with him, more time trying to make sure he took off his hat in class rather than teaching him advanced phonics and increasing his reading abilities. I had years of harmful mistakes with James. In retrospect, it is no wonder statistics class with me in particular tended to trigger him—frequently leading James to walk out of class and process my offenses with my female Special Education teacher counterpart. However, this Circle had hooked him. He spent every spare minute that Friday researching the mass incarceration of Black and Brown people in the US and asked if he could do an independent research project on the subject for extra credit.

When I reflect on my first Circle, I wonder what would have been different if I had taken the time to form a real relationship and build love and trust with my co-teacher prior to the lesson to understand his worldview, his assumptions, and to share mine. While I worry about the harm caused during this lesson, I also worry about the harm caused if I had instead decided to take over the conversation interrupting my co-teacher, wielding my power as a White male educator to boisterously refute, call out, and dominate my colleague while he held the talking piece. I also wonder how much better a teacher I would have been for James if I had the confidence and self-love at the time to be vulnerable, take more risks, take more responsibility for my mistakes, and be more honest on a daily basis. I wonder what would the outcomes for this lesson would have looked like if I shared my honest reflection when the talking piece got to me—still stating the counterstories to my co-worker (disrupting active racism), but also stating my personal errors in poorly preparing for this lesson, and asking the students how I might repair any harm caused during the lesson.

When I reflect on what a classroom-oriented toward social justice looks like, I think by definition there is no one method, there is no singular pedagogy, no sole curriculum, but there are forms of instruction that better embody social justice values and principles just as there are forms of instruction that better embody domination and hierarchy. What follows is a collection of pedagogies I have found to support spaces oriented toward social justice. But remember, if our beliefs, vision, purpose, values, and principles do not also align to social justice, any of these practices can easily be co-opted for dominance, oppression, and social reproduction.

Pedagogy

In *Justice by Design*, I use the term *pedagogy* to describe the specific teaching practices, strategies, or methods we can implement to bring our principles (the how) rooted in social justice to life in our curriculum. For example, *hows* like "be authentic" or "resist binaries and borders" are relatively vague in their direct realization in the classroom and our curriculum. I think of critical literacy as a pedagogy that can bring these principles (and more) to fruition, just as cooperative learning is a specific pedagogy that can bring the principle of building community (among others) to life.

In our current educational landscape, many pedagogies were created to support hierarchy and domination. For example, the practice of grading on a curve can only lead to competition and domination as it erodes community and *mattering*[35] within a classroom. The practice of lecturing nonstop only reinforces hierarchy as the teacher sits on top of a metaphorical pyramid of knowledge and stacks their students in rows beneath them, placing students with the "right" answers the "right" knowledge directly below them in the pyramid and relegating students with *othered* knowledge or ways of being to the bottom of the pyramid, in essence silencing and crushing them in one move. Think of the pedagogies of memorization or practicing and practicing

---

[35] See pages 95-98 for a discussion of mattering

procedures out of a real-world application that push students to be passive receptacles or computerized plug-in robots rather than empowered change makers.

Below is a short list I have found to be powerful in bringing many *hows* oriented toward social justice to life in curriculum writing. As with most lists in this book, this is not an exclusive, exhaustive, end-all be-all list. This is merely a list of practices and approaches I have found valuable that continues to grow as I learn new ways of teaching and as new ways of teaching are imagined or brought back to classrooms in our educational system. It is also not a hierarchical list; it is ordered in a way that makes it easier to share. Some may also use such pedagogies or variations of these pedagogies by different names. I find this list of practices and approaches useful when I am designing entire units, as a way to incorporate multiple methods over time, rather than using just one of these methods exclusively. Also remembering that curriculum oriented toward social justice moves beyond artificial borders between areas of study to create interdisciplinary curriculum, then by definition, all of these pedagogies can be incorporated into all areas of study.

(1) Critical Literacy, (2) Windows and Mirrors, (3) Storytelling for Social Justice, (4) Artistic Expression, (5) Somatics (6) Taking Action in the World, (7) Cooperative Learning, and (8) Talking Circles. Throughout this chapter, I strive to give a brief overview of each pedagogy, how it can relate to *Justice by Design*'s

guiding principles, and how it can be used to develop curriculum oriented toward social justice. While reviewing these pedagogies, note how many can be used simultaneously, or intertwined into a cohesive unit.

Critical Literacy

Paulo Freire (2018), the foundational figure for critical literacy, stated that students need to "Read the Word to Read the World." Through this quote, Freire demonstrates the power and purpose of literacy—to *read between the lines* of both text and society and sharpen our personal worldview in the process. (Note: the term *text* can include any medium through which individuals are communicating with each other such as a book, magazine, journal, song, show, commercial, or painting.)

Literacy in the twenty-first century needs to be more than the technical understanding of how to decode words, gain knowledge from texts, or share ideas through written and spoken language. In the twentieth century, literacy instruction should include both the above attributes, *and* literacy should empower scholars to analyze systems of oppression along with their personal place and power within these systems through the presentation of multiple perspectives, questioning of mind, and context.

All sources reflect the perspectives and biases of their authors. Collectively texts can amplify some voices, while silencing or marginalizing others. Central to critical literacy is understanding whose voice is included, whose is left out, and why. The question of why always circles back to an analysis of power. Therefore, inherent to critical literacy is an analysis of oppressor-oppressed politics[36]. Through this analysis, critical literacy can also be used to reveal one's own subjective beliefs about the world by causing them to question their personal assumptions and stance throughout the process.

On the outside, critical literacy is about being critical of the perspectives and hidden agendas in a text. At a deeper level, critical literacy is about understanding systems of oppression through analysis, about deepening one's personal worldview and understanding of self. Coffey (2015) explains critical literacy as, "the ability to read texts in an active, reflective manner in order to better understand power, inequality, and injustice in human relationships." As discussed at numerous points in this book, an analysis of power, inequality, and injustice in human relationships should include personal reflection to gain a deeper understanding. In a sense, being critical is really about being aware: aware of the systems at play in the context of a text, aware of the lens used while creating a text, aware of one's personal lens interpreting a text. To unlock the power of critical literacy, teachers must be willing to

---

[36] See *Pedagogy of the Oppressed* by Paulo Freire (1998) for a detailed discussion of oppressor-oppressed politics.

create a space where all members of a classroom can engage in courageous conversations[37].

Teachers can facilitate the development of students' critical literacy by:

1. Naming systems of oppression to give students context and vocabulary to discuss injustices
2. Presenting students with multiple perspectives
3. Providing questions that push students to analyze texts for bias and underlying messages, and to see the power relations within those messages
4. Ask questions that require a student to relate underlying messages of power dynamics back to their own personal local and immediate self and surroundings.

For example, Agarwal-Rangnath et al. (2016) write, "When reading a text critically, a teacher might ask her students questions such as: Whose voice is heard? Whose is missing? Why are certain voices silenced in the text? Questions such as these teach students to examine texts for bias, including the Eurocentric viewpoint that is often promoted in textbooks. By incorporating multiple perspectives through multiple texts, students get the chance to see the many viewpoints of a given event." Taking this to the personal local and immediate world, the teacher could also ask: How does

---

[37] See page 222-223 for a brief summary of courageous conversations.

this relate to your experience? How does this relate to your beliefs? How does this make you feel?

Critical literacy also allows teachers to move beyond the false binary of either I am orienting my class toward social justice or I am using rigorous grade-level standards. Using critical literacy, a teacher must meet rigorous grade-level reading standards while pursuing deeper critical questioning. There are numerous supports and guides available to help facilitate critical literacy. I would suggest that for more information on the foundations of critical literacy one reads Paulo Freire if one has not already.

When used for the purpose (*The Why*) of social justice, as Paulo Freire initially intended, critical literacy can bring to life values such as authenticity, intersectionality, mattering, rigorous academic expectations, and taking a stance, while simultaneously preparing students for the realities of rigorous standardized tests—allowing educators to move past the binary of *either* social justice-oriented curriculum *or* rigorous curriculum. Critical literacy captures both/and. Building on the idea of introducing multiple perspectives in texts, and being critical of our worldview, we come to the critical pedagogy of Windows and Mirrors.

Windows and Mirrors

Guiding Question: How did you feel when you first saw yourself in a text?

In 1988, Emily Style, co-founder of SEED with Peggy McIntosh, educator, author, and self-identified White woman from a working-class background, wrote the essay entitled "Windows and Mirrors: Creating Reflective and Inclusive Classrooms." In the essay, she writes that we need, "Curriculum to function both as window and as mirror, in order to reflect and reveal most accurately both a multicultural world and the student herself or himself. If the student is understood as occupying a dwelling of self, education needs to enable the student to look through window frames in order to see the realities of others and into mirrors in order to see her/his own reality reflected. Knowledge of both types of framing is basic to a balanced education."

A mirror is a narrative that reflects one's own culture, while a window is a narrative that offers a view into someone else's experience. In the classroom, mirrors include *texts* (defined liberally as in the previous section) in which students can find themselves, their families, and their communities reflected and valued. This valuing helps students find a sense of belonging. Here, this pedagogy ties into culturally responsive teaching, which includes a range of practices that recognizes the importance of including students' cultural references in all aspects of learning from content to methods used (Ladson-Billings, 1994).

Windows include texts that support student's learning of how other people conduct themselves in the world. This helps students better understand how they might fit into the broader world. In the introduction to the *Storytelling Project* (2008), Bell et al. write, "As a multicultural society, the United States is rich with the stories of the diverse groups that make up this country. As a deeply racialized society, stained by structural racism, not all stories however are equally acknowledged, affirmed or valued. Many stories survive through tenacious resistance in the face of a status quo that marginalizes, and often silences, their telling thus diminishing their truths." Given that many stories have been marginalized in the US, depending on the diverse materials a teacher chooses to use, for some students, this may be their first exposure to differences in race, religion, nationality, culture, and lifestyle. Given this, it is crucial that the introduction of windows cultivate acceptance and not judgment. Using materials that break free from oppressive narratives and ensuring that materials ripe with bias are critically examined is key to supporting acceptance. Essential questions that support acceptance include asking students to consider what we lose when stories are concealed or lost, and what we gain when we listen to and learn from a diverse collection of stories, as well as asking students to make their own personal comparisons between others and self and discover personal similarities and differences.

An ultimate goal of a Windows and Mirrors pedagogy is to help students foster positive identity development and intercultural competencies. Therefore, it is important to remember that these goals represent a lifelong process and require regular reflection to shift. Don't expect students to know how to do this work on their own or to achieve movement overnight. In contemplating this, another strategy beyond asking open-ended questions that support metacognition (thinking about your thinking), is to use Howard Gardner's strategy from Harvard's Project Zero, which has students share: "I used to think X, but now I think Y."

Most interestingly, in Style's (1988) foundational essay, she noted that as students begin to listen to stories of others, "we can see our own image reflected in the glass of their window. The window becomes a mirror! And it is the shared humanity of our conversation that most impresses us even as we attend to our different frames of reference." Using a windows and mirrors pedagogy gives students access to narratives that reflect their own experience as well as the experiences of others to build an understanding of self and intercultural competencies. This pedagogy has the potential to reinforce authenticity, intersectionality, students mattering, resisting binaries and borders, and supporting hope, joy, and pleasure in the classroom. Exploring stories and narratives created by other people can be a meaningful pedagogy for social justice, just as creating one's own story can be.

Storytelling for Social Justice

Guiding Question: What stories from your life lead to a desire to write curriculum oriented toward social justice?

Stories are an integral part of the human experience. There is a reason we flock to movies all over the world, why our hearts race as a character embarks on a hero's journey, why we cry as we meet a grown-up Harry Potter saying goodbye to his sons Severus and Albus as they board the Hogwarts express in the epilogue of *The Deathly Hallows*, literally every time the scene approaches (*Oh that doesn't happen to you, just me?*). There is a reason it is so easy to find empathy for others in a story. Stories capture human attention because whatever is happening in a story is happening to us and not just *them*. It is through this power, this embodiment, that we can find motivation for action.

Paul VanDeCarr (2015), a self-identified gay White man writes in *Storytelling and Social Change*, "Story is sometimes described as a powerful 'tool,' and it certainly can be that. But for a moment, think of stories less as a discrete instrument or product and more as a fundamental aspect of human consciousness; they're an essential part of how we think, feel, remember, imagine, relate—and create change… Statistics and lists of facts can communicate information, but stories communicate meaning and emotion, which are what motivate people to act. People don't relate to issues, they relate to other people—in other words, to their stories. And once we understand one another, we can identify our shared vision for a better world and work to make it a reality. Besides, telling stories is fun and creative."

Storytelling is part of the human experience, and this has incredible power. It can be both a form of resistance and creation, a form of cage crushing and nest building. bell hooks (2003) reminds us that women of color have stories to tell, and the mere act of women of color telling their stories is an act of resistance. Aman Sium and Eric Ritske write in *Speaking truth to power: Indigenous storytelling as an act of living resistance* (2013), that, "Stories in Indigenous epistemologies are disruptive, sustaining, knowledge producing, and theory-in-action." For example, the authors describe that, "By telling our stories we're at the same time disrupting dominant notions of intellectual rigor and legitimacy, while also redefining scholarship as a process that begins with the self." Sium and Ritske go on to note that when, "stories are archives of collective pain, suffering and resistance, then to speak them is to heal; to believe in them is to reimagine the world." Ron Ritchhart (2015) adds the metaphor that culture itself is a story we tell, and as such, culture can be transmitted through storytelling. If we are to build our classroom culture around social justice, we must incorporate storytelling.

Telling stories can be a meaningful pedagogy for orienting your curriculum toward social justice by empowering students to create their own narratives, listen to each other's narratives, learn from each other, create empathy, dream, and motivate change. Lee

Anne Bell et al. (2008) articulate four different powerful forms or categories of stories for social justice in *The Storytelling Project Curriculum*: Stock Stories, Concealed Stories, Resistance Stories, and Counter Stories. Stock stories are the most public and ubiquitous stories generally functioning to maintain the status quo. Concealed stories are those circulated by people who have been marginalized that are often hidden to dominant groups. Resistance stories may be historical or contemporary and challenge the stock stories. Finally, counter stories or transformative-emergent stories are, "new stories that are deliberately constructed to challenge the stock stories, build on and amplify resistance stories, and offer ways to interrupt the status quo and work for change."

Through this pedagogy, students can simultaneously learn and practice using the ingredients of good storytelling such as including a strong hook, engaging protagonists, relevant obstacles, meaningful settings, a turning point or climax, falling action, resolution, and a clear essence or meaning. In certain iterations, this method can be intertwined with figurative language, metaphors, and complex imagery. Using this pedagogy while maintaining high expectations for students' creations has the potential of creating incredibly meaningful and rigorous assignments.

Some potentially meaningful examples of story ideas adapted from *Storytelling and Social Change* (VanDeCarr, 2015), Sheila Arnold, and the Pacific Education Group include:

Title	Prompt
Intersectional Identity-Based Autobiographies	Ask students to write their racial, gender, class, sexuality, ability, nationality, language, or intersectional autobiographies. For an example adapted from Pacific Education Group: racial autobiographies can start with prompts like: What was your first personal experience in dealing with race or racism? Describe what happened. Describe your most recent personal experience in dealing with race or racism. Describe what happened. Similarly prompts are then used to have students focus on their family background, neighborhood, and schooling. One can also change *race* for other identity markers to support students in building other identity-based autobiographies.
A Story of Self	Ask students to tell a story that describes why they want to work for social justice.
A Story of Us	Ask a group of students to tell a story of the group coming together to work for social justice.
A Story of Now	Ask students to tell a personal story about a problem facing their community now.
A Success Story	Ask students to share a story where they felt success in the struggle for social justice.

A Failure Story	Ask students to share a story where they failed, possibly where they failed in the pursuit of social justice, and how can they hug that failure (see chapter 13 for more on hugging failures). Or ask students to share a story of how an individual failed to dominate and oppress and the learning for social justice that came from the failure.
A Values Story	Ask students to share a story that epitomizes a core value or principle of theirs that relates to social justice (look at part II for examples of core values related to social justice).
Alternative Histories	Ask students to pick a moment in history where they might intervene to create a new more socially just timeline.
Superpowers	Ask students to create a superhero story where the superhero(s) powers are used to fight injustice. Powers may even come from perceived marginalized identity characteristics.
Ghost Stories or Monster Stories	Ask students to create a ghost or monster story where the antagonist is the personification of some injustice. For example, maybe the "monster" is White supremacy as in the movie *Get Out*.
Animal Kingdom	Ask students to create a story where talking animals or plant qualities embody forces for social justice. Think of dandelions that embody community and healing.

Detectives	Ask students to create a detective story where the protagonist attempts to solve a social justice problem or mystery.
New Rules	Ask students to create a story where they change one law or social code and explore what happens.
Parables	Have students start a story with a parable related to social justice, and then tell a personal story that exemplifies the parable.
Mythology or Fairy Tales	Ask students to create a myth or fairy tale where they explore an injustice or empowerment related to social justice. Or have students modify a well-known myth or fairy tale to retell it from a new perspective that supports social justice. Or have students tell a personal or modern parallel story to a well-known myth or fairy tale that exemplifies social justice.

This list is meant to spark ideas for meaningful projects and assessments for curriculum oriented toward social justice. For more on storytelling for social justice read *Storytelling and Social Change* by Paul VanDeCarr (2015), Pacific Education Groups Racial Autobiographies, or look up workshops by Sheila Arnold (http://www.mssheila.org/), among many other great resources out there. In chapter 11 on assessment, we will dive deeper into how one can incorporate such practices into a cohesive unit plan. Such creative projects can also extend well beyond storytelling.

Artistic Expression

Beyond storytelling, creativity, imagination, and art more generally are critical to social justice. Creativity, often reinforced by all forms of artistic expression, allows us to imagine a path toward a socially just future that has yet to be imagined. And art, artistic expression in all its forms, has always been at the center of creativity. Art supports hope and joy by creating space to imagine the impossible and by reinforcing that students' personal expression and culture matter. Dr. Bettina Love (2019) exemplifies this as she writes, "Writing, drawing, acting, painting, composing, spittin' rhymes, and/or dancing is love, joy, and resistance personified." Dr. Love shares that artistic expression is integral to how children who identify as BIPOC make sense of injustice and thrive. Dr. Love teaches us that artistic expression is integral to creating a better world, and that art which meets this ideal must be, "rooted in intense design, research, and musings for justice."

Contrary to these assertions, in so many schools, art is one of the first programs cut for budgetary reasons, or when decisions are made to focus on increasing test scores in reading, math, and science. Art is so often perceived as separate from other areas of study, separate and often less than other areas of study. Yet artistic expression runs through all subject matter: think of the sheer beauty in images of radioactively tagged microscopic neurons interacting, the melodic sounds from words put to paper, or the depictions of geometric self-portraits that capture authentic self-expression. Powerful artistic expression that orients toward social justice personifies the highest levels of academic rigor—combining rigor found in multiple disciplines.

Dr. Emdin, who started the #HipHopEd movement[38] notes that using art in academic spaces raises the level of rigor, as high expectations become critical to the creative process. Dr. Emdin (2017) writes it is important for educators to position, "Art and aesthetics as central to teaching and learning even though they are too often relegated to being extracurricular." In this vein, Dr. Emdin goes on to argue that rigor is raised and students think more deeply when we identify, "Phenomena that emotionally connects or motivates the student, and that the most significant emotional connections we have are to the art we consume and the most powerful and healthy emotional releases we have is through this art we create." Dr. Emdin notes that while using the vast artistic elements intertwined with hip-hop in a classroom context such as science, teachers must hold high expectations for students' expressions and understanding grade-level content. This gets back to Dr. Love's words that art, which inspires for social justice, must incorporate *intense design, research, and musings for justice.*

---

[38] The #HipHopEd movement strives to use hip-hop as text, theory, philosophy, and practice for interventions in areas of science, technology, engineering, mathematics, counseling/therapy, literacy, and school leadership.

While Dr. Emdin uses the vast artistic elements found in hip-hop to create more socially just classrooms, there are also powerful instances of teachers using other verbal, visual, and dramatized artistic expressions to support classrooms oriented toward social justice. In *Preparing to Teach Social Studies for Social Justice* (Agarwal-Rangnath, 2016), the authors describe how Brian, a 10th-grade US history teacher, uses drama and acting (via a character-driven seminar[39]) to teach about the French Revolution, leading students to discuss and experience the essential question: How do we stop the cycle of revolution?

In listening to teachers across nineteen states, Bellisario and Donovan (2012) found that integrating the arts into their disciplines: (1) leads to deep learning, increased student ownership, and engagement with academic content; (2) provides a variety of strategies for accessing content and expressing understanding; (3) creates learning that is culturally responsive and relevant in students' lives; (4) engages students in twenty-first-century skills including creativity, innovation, and imagination; and (5) develops empathy, awareness of multiple perspectives, and cultural sensitivity to others. Given the power of the arts, there are

---

[39] An essential question-driven discussion that is run by seminar rules in which students are assigned a point of view, usually an historical figure. The purpose of the discussion is for students to argue about the essential question from a particular point of view.

a wide variety of resources available to support teachers in incorporating the arts in interdisciplinary classrooms.

Incorporating a student's artistic expression with high expectations and social justice goals into any of our disciplines can be a powerful way to support authenticity, hope, joy, pleasure, mattering, demanding the impossible, and building bridges.

Another pedagogy that supports us in connecting to our authentic emotional selves is somatics.

Somatics

What did you feel when you watched firsthand or heard about George Floyd's murder in Minneapolis, crying out to his dead mother as a White male police officer pinned George to the ground and drove his knee into George's neck for over eight minutes, killing him? What did you feel when you learned about LatinX children separated from loved ones and locked in cages with other babies upon crossing the Mexico–US border? What did you feel when the US government broke yet another treaty with Native Americans to run the Dakota access pipeline through Dakota land to maximize profits for oil companies?

Where did you feel each of these atrocities? Your stomach? Adrenal glands? The back of your throat? Your heart? The palms of your hands? Your legs? Your feet? Your skin? If you were not directly connected, did you feel the physical pain of those who were? Did you personally feel the visceral anguish in George

Floyd's last breaths or the fear in LatinX babies crying alone in a holding facility? If you felt nothing, did you actually engage your whole being in understanding the circumstances?

Rea Johnson (2018), a self-identified queer scholar working at the intersection of somatic studies and social justice notes in *Embodied Social Justice* that somatic pedagogies incorporate presence, somatic literacy, and kinesthetic empathy. These terms are defined below:

- **Presence**: The ability to attend to the sight, sound, touch, pain, pressure, temperature, itch, visceral sensations, fatigue, hunger, and thirst of oneself, peers, and the environment.
- **Somatic Literacy**: The ability to access knowledge encoded in kinesthetic and nonverbal material. This form of literacy supports knowing what is grounded in embodied experience. It allows us to access and use what we know in our bones.
- **Kinesthetic Empathy**: The willingness and capacity to imagine viscerally in our own bodies what might be occurring in the body of another.

In understanding the above-mentioned atrocities, were you present? Could you read the situation in your bones? Could you tap into kinesthetic empathy?

Somatics is an embodiment of moving beyond binaries and artificial borders to find our authentic selves—it strives to reconnect the body with the mind, allowing for powerful healing and powerful change. Generative Somatics (2006), an organized network of politicized somatic coaches, therapists, and healing practitioners write, "The word somatics comes from the Greek root soma, which means 'the living organism in its wholeness.' It is the best word we have in English to understand human beings as an integrated mind/body/spirit, and as social, relational beings... Somatics is a path, a methodology, and a change theory by which we can embody transformation, individually and collectively." Somatics supports us and our students in aligning our values and actions with our entire being. In other words, somatics supports us to fully embody our intentions, our *whys,* our beliefs, and our values for social justice.

Despite the power of engaging our bodies in learning and unlearning, Rea Johnson (2018) writes, "One of the most resounding silences in educational theories, pedagogical practices, and institutional structures [has] to do with the body. Traditional schooling largely ignores the body, except to address it as a possession that must be properly maintained."

While somatics is a newer area of focus in education, "mindfulness" and "grounding in" are practices that have existed in some capacity in P12 education for some time, and that can relate to *presence*. Additionally, many methods from the performing arts and physical education may incorporate practices that more closely align to somatic pedagogies. However, it is clear there needs to be more work done on elucidating practices in this area to extend somatic methods to all classrooms.

Generative Somatics (2006) also notes that somatics is more than adding "body-based" exercises to our classrooms, more than bringing our attention to our bodies and sensations. Generative Somatics writes, "we are not mind over matter (if only I think differently I will be different), nor matter over mind or spirit (a change in chemistry or medication will wholly change my experience). Rather, we are all of these things combined—we are thinking and conceptual, we are emotional, we are biological, we are spiritual, we are relational and we are social. Somatics approaches people as this integrated whole, working with these interdependent aspects of who we are."

Somatics can and should be combined with the other pedagogies on this list. By harnessing the power of ours and our students' full selves, whole being, mind, body, and soul, we create the capacity for lasting social justice, for deconstructing oppressive cages in and outside of ourselves, and creating loving, interdependent nests with the bodies and minds of those surrounding us. We create the capacity for meaningful action.

Taking Action in the World

Being critical of our world, ourselves, exploring creativity and imagining, and sharing our stories in listening to others are all important and ideally naturally lead toward action. While understanding and rebuilding our personal identities, how could we just observe inequities in our communities without taking action? In orienting our curriculum toward social justice, we must include pedagogies that create space for students to take action. Agarwal-Rangnath et al. (2016) write that teachers working for social justice, "Create opportunities for their students to work for social change. In particular, social justice teachers encourage students to work for the rights of those who are dominated or marginalized, through the creation of student-led activist clubs, through action research projects that focus on issues in their community and across the globe and possible solutions, and through well-crafted service learning opportunities."

We will cover understandings and assessments related to taking action for social justice in chapters 12 and 13, but for now, let's focus on one method to take action in the world that has received considerable attention globally: Youth Participatory Action Research. Now, before jumping into this, think about what happens to research when the researched become the researcher?

Youth Participatory Action Research: is a process where students and adults partner to improve the conditions of youth lives and communities using participatory action research techniques. The goal of such research is to empower youth to advocate for change in their communities. In this process, youth are valuable experts, implying a shared power between youth and adults. However, adults should still support structuring the process to help ensure youth receive strong training and skills.

Through Youth Participatory Action Research, classrooms can redefine who has the expertise to produce knowledge in the world, provide skills in inquiry, evidence, and presentation to students, while simultaneously providing communities change agents from within, as well as evaluating programs, policies, and practices that affect young people. This process directly empowers students to be agents of change.

To these ends, this process can help demonstrate that students matter; help students and teachers hone an intersectional worldview; hold high expectations for students through inquiry, evidence, and presentation skill development; and continue to foster community.

There are numerous books and support available for facilitating Youth Participatory Action Research; in particular, YPAR (Youth-led Participatory Action Research) at berkeley.edu offers great lesson plans and guidance to facilitate Youth Participatory Action Research free of charge. And just like so many of the other pedagogies discussed in this chapter, this process can be combined with critical literacy, windows and mirrors, storytelling, artistic expression, and the next section: cooperative learning.

Cooperative Learning

In the classroom, students and teachers are placed in close proximity to one another. The promise of placing people with diverse backgrounds (whether referring to racial, socioeconomic, sexual, linguistic, national origin, ethnic, religious, or other cultural diversity) has the potential to increase positive relationships, empathy, and new creative imaginations while decreasing biases. However, merely placing groups of people together does not mean they will work cooperatively. The Johnson brothers (2002), two White men and fierce lifelong advocates of cooperative learning, write, "Proximity is a necessary condition for the positive potential of diversity to be realized, but it is not sufficient in and of itself. The promise of diversity is that it will enrich and enhance relationships, productivity, and other important outcomes. There is a risk, however, that diversity will lead to negative rather than positive outcomes... with actual contact stereotypes can be confirmed and expanded, and prejudice can be strengthened. Direct interaction among diverse individuals in competitive and individualistic situations can create negative relationships characterized by hostility, rejection, divisiveness, scapegoating, bullying, stereotyping, and prejudice." The authors argue only in an environment structured for cooperative learning can we guarantee the promises of diversity.

The Johnson brothers divide classroom relational experiences into three distinct categories: competitive, individualistic, and cooperative. In the competitive experience, there is negative interdependence meaning students can only succeed if their peers fail. In the individualistic experience, there is no interdependence meaning one student's success has no bearing on another student's success. In the cooperative experience, there is positive interdependence meaning students can only succeed if their peers succeed. The Johnson brothers note that while all three experiences hold value (competition for fun in small amounts, individualistic for accountability in small amounts) the majority of class time should focus on cooperative learning experiences to both build stronger academic gains and a connected community. However, in the US, the vast majority of class time is structured as independent experiences as discussed in chapter 5. Historically, a push for individuality in the classroom is a rather new prerogative, only 100 plus years old, while cooperative learning methods have been pushed by societies around the globe for the past two thousand years (Johnson et al., 2008).

To create more cooperative experiences, teachers must intentionally structure positive interdependence, by leading students to believe the only way they can succeed is if their peers succeed. Structuring positive independence can be done in several ways, including providing students with separate roles, a group identity, tasks that require every student's input (a jigsaw activity where each group only has a piece of the information they need to share to understand all the information), limited resources (just one canvas to create a shared painting), or group contingent rewards (if all students in the class get 80 percent or higher on their assessment, all students get five extra bonus points).

The Johnson brothers (2008) note that every lesson should have a cooperative learning objective in addition to content and/or skill objectives, or intertwined with content and skill lesson objectives. In addition to intentionally structuring positive interdependence, which the Johnson brothers note is the most important requirement for cooperative learning, they also share four other important elements, which include individual and group accountability, promotive interaction (like sharing resources, support, and praise), teaching leadership skills, and group processing. Below is a list of potential cooperative learning activities where positive interdependence is explicitly structured.

A Short List of Cooperative Learning Activities	
Jigsaw	In this cooperative learning strategy, students are divided into groups and assignments/readings/information are broken into pieces. Each member of the group is given just one piece of the assignment/reading/information. The group must then work together (dependent on each other) to complete putting together the puzzle or *jigsaw*.
Think-Pair-Share	In this cooperative learning strategy, students work together to solve a problem or answer a question about an assignment/reading. This

	strategy requires students to (1) think individually about a topic or answer to a question, and (2) share ideas with a peer. After sharing with a peer, one can often have students share with the entire group.
Pair Reading	In this cooperative learning strategy, two students work together to read an assigned text. Students can be given directions, such as Partner A reads the first paragraph, and then Partner B verbally summarizes the first paragraph. Next, Partner B reads the second paragraph, and then Partner A summarizes it. This can also be used for repeated reading fluency exercises where students take several turns reading a passage fluently and timing each other.
Writing Editors	In this cooperative learning strategy, students receive feedback from their peers about the quality and clarity of writing assignments. This strategy generally has three parts. First, critically reading a peer's writing and generating comments to be shared. Second, during class, students review comments provided by their peers and have the opportunity for clarification. Third, students can bring unresolved questions and issues to a broader class discussion.
Constructive Controversy	In this cooperative learning strategy, students are put into groups of four or pairs and are given an issue on which to write a report. One-half of the group is given the "con" position on the issue and the other half is given the "pro" position. The cooperative goal of reaching a consensus on the issue and writing a quality group report is highlighted. Students

	then begin by researching their assigned position (generally outside of class). In class, they share and advocate for their assigned position within their group. Next, students reverse their position and advocate for the other side's position. Finally, groups synthesize assertions from both sides of the controversy and come to consensus.
Base Groups	Cooperative base groups are long-term, stable groups that last for the duration of a course, or even years. These groups generally contain 3–5 individuals with different aptitudes and perspectives. They provide a context in which students can support each other in academics as well as in other aspects of their lives. The group members make sure everyone is completing their work and hold each other accountable for their contributions.

For more information facilitating cooperative learning read Cooperation in the Classroom by Johnson et al. (2008).

This pedagogy can be combined with most other pedagogies; for example, critical literacy tasks can easily be turned into cooperative group activities, just as windows and mirrors, storytelling, and other artistically expressive tasks can.

Talking Circles

Talking Circles are old. Really, really old. There is evidence that Indigenous people around the world have used Circle processes for thousands of years (Living Justice Press, n.d.). The

Circle pedagogy discussed here is rooted in the tradition of talking Circles that Indigenous peoples in North America use and have used for millennia. In my personal experience, the process taught to me was passed down from the teachings of elders of both the Ojibwe and Lakota in the upper Midwest of the US.

Circles began entering US K-12 pedagogy on a large scale via restorative justice practices and feminist movements over the past thirty years. For example, First Nations in Canada started teaching the Circle practice to non-Native people to find alternatives to the mass incarceration of their people in the 1990s. Using Indigenous practices to resolve conflicts and support healing required collaboration with non-Native people. In the process, non-Native people experienced the Circle process and its power to bring positive transformation for everyone involved (Living Justice Press, n.d.). Today, Circles are integral to the framework for restorative justice. From origins like these, the use of Circles among non-Native people has continued to grow in schools throughout North America.

In general, the Circle process establishes a very different style of communication from traditional Eurocentric forms of communication that prevail in K-12 education. Instead of using aggressive debate and hierarchies of knowledge, often leading to only a select group of assertive individuals participating fully, the Circle process creates a safe nonhierarchical space in which all present have the opportunity to speak without interruptions.

Circle processes are based upon equality between participants and the principle of sharing power and knowledge instead of attempting to dominate others or hold power over one another.

Rather than active verbal facilitation in a more hierarchical discussion, communication is regulated through the passing of a talking piece (an object of special meaning or symbolism to the Circle facilitator who is usually called the Circle keeper). The talking piece supports listening and reflection because both are important to mutual understanding laying the groundwork for deeper, more meaningful discussion.

Circles generally begin with brief opening comments by the Circle keeper about the purpose of the Circle, listing of ground rules, and asking for additional contributions to the ground rules. Then the Circle keeper can pose a question and pass the talking piece (traditionally to the person on the left, clockwise). Only the person with the talking piece can speak. If others jump in with comments, the Circle keeper reminds them of the ground rules and refocuses on the person with the talking piece. Participants are not required to speak because this may create an unsafe, pressured tone to the Circle. If someone does not feel the desire or ability to speak, they can simply pass the talking piece to the next person.

Circles both require and build on trust in a classroom community, and once self-love and trust are in abundance, Circles have the power to ignite courageous acts of sharing. Alaina Winters (n.d.) shares that such acts can involve sharing potentially stigmatizing information such as identifying racism in the classroom to sharing traumatizing personal experiences. Winters (n.d.) writes, "From using talking circles I have learned that, when students are encouraged to be full human beings in the classroom instead of just students, courageous acts of sharing often profoundly impact the roots of the classroom community and can deepen the trust that makes all kinds of wonderful things possible."

In one example of wonderful things made possible, SEED describes an exercise named serial testimony that incorporates a Circle where participants speak about their experiences (not opinions), in turn, around a Circle and refrain from responding to what others have said. One hope of the exercise is that through hearing each other, participants also learn more about themselves (think back to our Windows and Mirrors). One of SEED's trainers, Chris Avery notes "[When students become] the experts ... it's amazing how much more they're willing to learn. ... When they understand that their thoughts are valued because they are their thoughts and not because they said the smartest thing or the most incredible thing ... you start to get more authentic thought" (Van Der Valk, 2014). Here, authentic thought allows students and teachers to come to deeper, personalized understandings of themselves and the world around them.

Depending on the questions asked, Circle discussions can provide a space for all participants (teachers and students included) to be experts, for participants to build new connections to each other and the content of the course, to dive deep and get critical of personal experiences, to listen to and share stories for justice, or solve problems together. Circles embody many aspects of this book's *hows* in pursuit of social justice: authenticity, intersectionality, making students matter, building community, building bridges, taking a stance, personal accountability, and discovering hope, joy, and pleasure.

Putting Our Pedagogies Together

As discussed throughout this chapter, so many of these pedagogies can be combined within the context of a single classroom. One can use critical literacy questioning techniques with texts that provide both windows and mirrors, within the midst of a cooperative learning exercise. Students can follow up the readings of integral texts by writing their own stories, creating their own artistically expressive projects, or by conducting action-oriented research. Students can reflect on how content affects them and others physically, learning *somatic literacy* and *kinesthetic empathy*, as well as harness mindfulness to be fully present through difficult course work. Students can culminate a unit with a Circle discussion of how their thinking might have changed or on how a window became a mirror. The possibilities are endless, and there are other variations of the pedagogies listed here and other entirely new pedagogies yet to be imagined that may be just as, or more, valuable to incorporate.

The key with implementing any strategy oriented toward social justice is to keep in mind the ultimate intentions of the pedagogy and how it is implemented. For example, I have personally implemented Circles in an unjust manner on multiple occasions. At one point in my career (years after the introductory narrative to this chapter), I would use my authority in the classroom to force students to respond to a prompt during a "Circle." I think even more damaging, at one time in my practice, I even rated students' Circle responses on a scale of 1 to 3 based on oral presentation skills I was working on with them at the time. In both of these instances, I went against sacred aspects of the Circle, such as creating a safe space, sharing power, and sharing who can be the keeper of knowledge. And yet at the time, I thought I was doing the work of social justice with exquisite execution by using weekly "Circles" in my practice (I quoted Circles in these examples because how I enacted them meant they could not be considered Circles). I share this to show how easy it is to fall back into the noxious and intoxicating fumes of hierarchies and power hoarding if we are not very intentionally resisting them.

To help guide us in our intentions, I propose using backward planning as a valuable process in designing curriculum oriented toward social justice.

Recap and Moving Forward

Any pedagogy can be co-opted for injustice. Just by using a strategy previously discussed does not mean it is being used as a tool for social justice. I have fallen prey to thinking I was *woke*[40] when in truth I may have been doing more harm than good on numerous occasions. While any pedagogy can be oriented toward oppression, some strive to bend toward social justice. Examples I have found in this realm include: critical literacy, windows and mirrors, storytelling for social justice, artistic expression, somatics, participatory youth action research, cooperative learning, and talking Circles. Some questions that can help frame choosing using more socially just pedagogies include:

1. Why am I choosing to use this pedagogy in my design?
2. How do I believe this pedagogy will facilitate the outcomes we wish to see in this unit (discussed in chapters 12 and 13)?
3. If I am not clear on the purpose of the use of this pedagogy in my design, what could my desire to utilize it be rooted in? Performance action? Optics? Guilt?

These questions naturally lead us toward a backward planning framework.

---

[40] A political term referring to a perceived awareness of issues concerning social justice and racial justice, derived from African American vernacular.

Chapter 11

Backward Planning and Social Justice

Every system is perfectly designed to get the results it gets.

—ATTRIBUTED TO MULTIPLE AUTHORS (CONWAY & BATALDEN, 2015). *AND YES, YOU MAY HAVE READ THIS QUOTE OPENING CHAPTER 2*

Guiding Question: How do intentions and a *why* rooted in social justice relate to backward planning and curriculum design?

Narrative: Teaching Pre-Service Teachers

The first time I taught future teachers at the collegiate level, I thought this was my chance to do something different. I wasn't tied to a prescriptive curriculum. The licensure standards I needed to follow were connected to Special Education—and I lived and breathed the content. I assumed the rigor was a given—being an advanced-level college course for Special Education master's and undergraduate students.

It was a big shift from teaching high school Special Education to teaching at the university level.

It grew my ego, not that my ego needed much help, but here I was, this person with learning disabilities who was told time and again, "College isn't for everyone, Ian." I could not wait to prove myself.

I thought I had all the answers because there was no way my classroom would be an environment where I sat and went through Powerpoint slide after slide cramming information into each bullet. No way. My class would be exciting, filled with cooperative learning groups, and most importantly, activities. Lots of activities.

I had an activity for every topic. In fact, if I could not turn a topic into an array of engaging activities, I cut it down to one page of information and moved on. It was a class designed to prepare teachers to teach academic strategies to struggling learners. Rather than read about interventions, we enacted them. Rather than read about the components of a lesson plan, students wrote lesson plans in groups. It was a college classroom where you could not fall asleep—and no one ever did, despite running from 5:00 to 9:30 p.m. on Tuesday nights.

After my first year, I felt incredibly proud each time course reviews came out, and my class consistently ended with high marks, placing it well above the department averages on all scales, such as like rigor and usefulness. The only area I was ever marked low on was availability and responding to emails. Emails! (Imagine my fist shaking as I state one the banes of my existence, but I digress.)

So, given how well the class seemed to go and given the great feedback from students, I was always perplexed when final projects were turned in...and they were terrible. The final project required students to put together just four lesson plans with reflections geared to address a particular student's difficulties. It seemed like such an easy task in my mind, especially after the number of activities we did in class loosely related to this goal. Had I understood the tenets of backward planning, then I would not have been shocked, but I did not, so I was. Students were listening and participating, but they were not grasping what I thought they should. Learning seemed to end with each activity.

What was I doing wrong? How could I get so much engagement, how could I get so many good reviews, how could the class seem to go so well, and yet the final outputs showed my students were just not understanding the material to the level I expected from them?

To state a heavily repeated quote in this book: "Every system is perfectly designed to get the results it gets" (Conway & Batalden, 2015). My error was in my design.

What Is Backward Planning?

Backward planning helps to ensure you get to where you want to go. It is not a new idea; I am not planning to re-create the idea here and claim it in the name of one more White guy. The authors who elevated backward design to a common term and practice in education are Wiggins and McTighe (2008) in their seminal work, *Understanding by Design* (*UbD*; You might notice that their title is similar to the title of this book, hmmm…). For a really in-depth look at backward design and fantastic teacher tools, I suggest that you read *UbD*.

While Wiggins and McTighe (2008) helped promote backward design as a powerful method of curriculum design, they are also quick to note they did not invent the principles of backward design either. Backward design has been used for a long time in education, and much, much longer in the more general world of design work. The authors of *UbD* parallel backward design to the *ancient* design edict *form follows function*.

In the world of education, "function" correlates to the desired results or desired learning, and "form" correlates to the assessments and evidence of learning followed by one's instructional practices. Therefore, in backward design, how you assess and teach *follows* what you want your students to walk away with, and I would add what *you* want to walk away with (as we should learn alongside our students).

The authors of *UbD* note the two biggest issues of educational planning are (1) activity-oriented design and (2) coverage, as both stem from a lack of backward design strategy. Activity-oriented design focuses on engaging experiences, not ultimate learning goals, and therefore only builds deeper understanding accidentally, if at all. The narrative that started this chapter is an example of activity-oriented design. To answer my perplexity raised in the narrative: *What was going wrong with my college course curriculum?* I was planning instruction around activities not understanding.

At the other end of curriculum design issues, coverage focuses on covering content without any care for understanding—think of the teacher who drudges on page after page or slide after slide of content as students fail test after test. The authors of *UbD* (2008) write that without backward planning, "The approach is more 'by hope' than 'by design.' Such an approach ends up unwittingly being one that could be described like this: Throw some content and activities against the wall and hope some of it sticks." In other words, if we plan by starting with our instruction or plan to cover content rather than understanding, we are cultivating "Understanding by Chance," not design.

Put another way, if we plan for seemingly just and meaningful experiences without planning for deeper understandings, we are cultivating "Justice by Chance," and social justice is too important to leave to chance. In fact, when left to chance, it is more likely our work will be swept away in the current of the status quo. If we plan to merely tell our students what to know, how to think, to passively listen to the sage on the stage, we will not support critical thinkers, change makers, and a connected community oriented toward social justice.

Backward design is really about intention. It is less about a prescribed path to creation that dictates you must start your planning process with your desired outcomes and then design from there. Rather, it is about ensuring that after you are done planning, what you teach aligns with what you assess, which aligns with your deeper intentions.

As discussed throughout this book, orienting curriculum toward social justice needs intentionality. There are too many intertwining systems of oppression working diligently in the White supremacist capitalist patriarchy.

As we see daily, White supremacy kills: it kills Black children with bullets "justifiably" shot from officers' guns, it kills LatinX children ripped from their parents and detained, it kills all groups of people whose use of drugs to numb the pain has skyrocketed. As we see daily, capitalism kills: it kills as corporations exploit "others'" children's labor around the globe, it kills as companies poison our drinking water, it kills as greenhouse gasses continue to raise our planet's temperature creating cataclysmic weather. As we see daily, patriarchy kills: it kills people sitting in desks at school or in pews at church as 99 percent of public mass murderers are male, it kills women in toxic relationships with toxic males and men committing suicide at higher rates in toxic relationships with themselves. The White supremacist capitalist patriarchy kills all of us. We need curriculum intentionally designed for social justice to support the deconstruction of these systems and build positive self-identities and realities.

Such education should feel good. Education oriented toward social justice should feel like the most pleasurable education there is. But we only get there, we only know we've gotten there, know whether we are achieving socially just deep understandings in the classroom, if we backward design to reach our shared goals. Using backward design can simultaneously free us to really focus on our students and live in the moment in our classrooms.

Using backward design is not to say that because we plan our curriculum to be goal oriented we lose focus on the *now* in our classrooms. The *now* is too important to lose focus on. As hooks (2003) writes, "Teaching students to be fully present, enjoying the moment, the Now in the classroom without fearing that this places the future in jeopardy: that is essential mindfulness practice for a true teacher. Without a focus on the 'Now' we can do the work of educating in such a way that we draw out all that is exquisite in our classroom, not just now and then, or at special moments, but always." While it may seem counterintuitive, by using backward design, we are better equipped to focus on enjoying the moment and being present in class with students because we have already done the work to think through our goals and process. Backward design allows us to enrich our time with students in the moment.

Backward design helps us educators focus on the outputs and purpose, rather than inputs. Input might be considered: What am I going to teach today? This shift in thinking is really important, since all too often we jump to the inputs. And yes, inputs can be more fun to plan; or we may be against deadlines (such as what am

I teaching next hour!#$@?) and be forced to focus on inputs asap; or we may not think we have the expertise to choose the outputs and therefore just skip that step and focus on inputs; or we may never have been taught to start with the outputs in the first place. As a teacher, I have lived each of these detours at some point in time. Wiggins and McTighe (2008) share an interesting perspective on the matter: "To put it in an odd way, too many teachers focus on the teaching and not the learning. They spend most of their time thinking, first, about what they will do, what materials they will use, and what they will ask students to do rather than first considering what the learner will need in order to accomplish the learning goals." I often mistakenly focus on the teaching and not the learning, but thankfully, there is support to shift our focus.

Backward Design in Practice

As laid out in *UbD*, backward design entails three stages:

Stage 1: Identify desired results.

Stage 2: Determine acceptable evidence.

Stage 3: Plan learning experiences and instruction.

To build on these stages, adding one, and orienting these stages more directly toward social justice, we can include the following details to each:

Stage 0: Do Your Self-Work and look in the mirror honestly and lovingly. Recognize and align your guiding intentions—your *why* and your *how* with your *what* (see chapters 1–7 and 14).

Stage 1: Identify desired results requires intertwining high rigor content, as gagged by grade-level standards, with relevant social justice content to create enduring understandings and essential questions for social justice. Chapter 9 of this book reviews how to ensure grade-level rigor, and chapter 13 addresses how to create enduring understandings and essential questions for social justice that open the door to rigorous content.

Stage 2: Determine acceptable evidence, we must ask what assessment methods capture the ambitious goals of deep enduring understandings of social justice (covered in chapter 13).

Stage 3: Plan learning experiences and instruction that meet our goals means using pedagogies oriented toward justice (covered in chapter 11), as education for social justice is both a *how* and a *what*.

To return to my opening narrative, had I used these tenets of backward design earlier on in my college course, I would have come to my final classroom set up much faster. By my fourth year as an adjunct professor for this strategies course, I redesigned the classroom into a completely flipped model where students completed content reviews at home, and then worked on putting their learning into practice in the classroom in cooperative groups.

While in groups or pairs, students received immediate and constant feedback from myself and peers while lesson planning.

With this shift, the class was no longer activity driven, though class time was virtually 100 percent activity based. The class was not designed around activities; rather, it was designed around the goals of learning how to build scaffolds and supports while lesson planning for students with disabilities—it just so happened I believed the best way to achieve these goals was through group activities that incorporated constant practice, feedback, and revision. My focus shifted to outcomes: What are students producing now, and what feedback do they need to produce something better?

During class time, students worked countless hours on their final projects, where they could receive immediate feedback on their work. Simultaneously, I used cooperative learning structures and had students in groups for most of class—removing my voice from all group instruction. I used my voice for key feedback, guiding students as they created lesson plans I could never have imagined! By the time final projects came around, students finally met the high standards and rigor I held for future educators. I only wish it hadn't taken me years and years to get to this point, especially as I think about the countless teachers I failed to prepare and the K-12 student impact this potentially had. Luckily, I was not preparing these teachers alone, and I like to think their other professors helped fill in the voids I left.

So how do you know if you are on the right track, if you are driven by activities or content or understanding, if you have chosen meaningful understandings, or the best path to reach said understandings?

Some questions to help you focus your process are provided below:

1. Who can I collaborate with who can help me see and address my blind spots when thinking about the end goals and outputs for my instruction?
2. How will we distinguish merely interesting learning from learning relevant and necessary for social justice?
3. What does it look like to meet the class's end goals and how does this align with my students and my own personal goals?
4. How can I hold myself accountable to my students' learning?
5. Whose voice is missing from the process?

The first and last questions are particularly important because they directly address our biases. We all hold biases. It is part of being human. To restate Dr. Sue's (2010) words, "Because most of us consciously experience ourselves as good, moral and decent human beings, the realization that we hold a biased worldview is very disturbing; thus we prefer to deny, diminish or avoid looking at ourselves honestly. Yet, research suggests that none of us are immune from inheriting the racial, gender, and sexual orientation biases of our society." Our biases can manifest themselves through instructional choices, such as the soft bigotry of low expectations, to building curriculum that only focuses on oppression and dismantling cages, rather than on building nests and empowering people who have been marginalized. If we make instructional choices in a vacuum, our personal worldviews of inclusion/exclusion, superiority/inferiority, normality/abnormality, and desirability/undesirability can go unchallenged—and inadvertently reinforce marginalization despite all the "good intentions" in our hearts.

In truth, the preceding "focusing" questions may actually open the door to more questions and thinking rather than focusing your process, but that is the beauty of true, messy design work. Rethinking your instruction, questioning your pedagogy, and working collaboratively generally means you are on the right path, though the work may get messy and lead to several iterations.

Recap and Moving Forward

To answer the guiding question: How do intentions and a *why* rooted in social justice relate to backward planning and curriculum design? If you don't utilize backward design, then students grasping deep understandings is a long shot, and social justice education is too important and too pleasurable to leave to chance. It needs educators to follow the ideas outlined in backward design: (1) know your desired outcomes that allow you to intertwine rigor and deep enduring understandings for social justice, (2) build evidence for desired outcomes that support scholars in crushing cages and building nests, and (3) plan instruction using pedagogies oriented toward social justice. Another way to think about it, our first design constraints are our deep enduring understandings for social justice that connect to grade-level standards, our second constraint is the outputs we are leading toward (change agents who understand how to crush cages and build nests), and our third constraint is our pedagogy—are we teaching in a socially just manner? Finally, constantly question your design constraints, making sure to collaborate with individuals who can help you mitigate your blind spots and reduce your biases.

Know, too, that while this process is set up to help you get to where you want to go, due to the iterative nature of both design work and social justice, accept that you may likely end up adapting where you want to go and reimagining your curriculum year after year, or even from your first period of the day to your last class. But that is progress.

Chapter 12

Understanding for Social Justice

The more that you read, the more things you will know. The more that you learn, the more places you'll go.

— Dr. Seuss (1990)

It is not enough to teach man a specialty. Through it he may become a kind of useful machine, but not a harmoniously developed personality. It is essential that the student acquire an understanding of and a lively feeling for values. He must acquire a vivid sense of the beautiful and of the morally good. Otherwise he—with his specialized knowledge—more closely resembles a well-trained dog than a harmoniously developed person.

— Albert Einstein (1952)

Our bodies have a form of knowledge that is different from our cognitive brains. This knowledge is typically experienced as a felt sense of constriction or expansion, pain or ease, energy or numbness. Often this knowledge is stored in our bodies as wordless stories about what is safe and what is dangerous. The body is where we fear, hope, and react; where we constrict and release; and where we reflexively fight, flee, or freeze. If we are to upend the status quo of white-body supremacy, we must begin with our bodies.

— Resmaa Menakem (2017)

People will forget what you said, people will forget what you did, but people will never forget how you made them feel.

— Attributed to multiple authors (Quote Research, 2014)

Essential Questions: What is the difference between *knowing* and *understanding*? What is the connection between *transfer* and *social justice*?

Narrative: A Breakthrough

"Does anyone have any real breakthroughs they are having at this moment to share with the group?" Glenn Singleton asked our room full of participants.

Glenn Singleton is the architect behind *Courageous Conversations for Race* (a foundational text and protocol for addressing race, racism, and Whiteness in the classroom or workplace), and founder of the Pacific Education Group (one of the world's largest racial equity consulting firms). Glenn Singleton is a visionary in the realm of racial equity and social justice, and identifies as a Black man. I was fortunate to be in a session he was cofacilitating on the history of the Civil Rights Movement in the 1960s that paralleled the work of Martin Luther King Jr. and Lyndon B. Johnson to current racial equity movements.

"I am talking about real breakthroughs," he reiterated as he walked between our tables. I did not raise my hand. I did not raise my voice. I did not share my breakthrough with the group, though I felt I was having a breakthrough in understanding racial equity at that very moment.

As a White man, I try not to take up too much of a group's limited verbal processing time in spaces with BIPOC and women or non-binary folk. Us White men get plenty of White male narrative time elsewhere (just look at this book). I have participated or led many White affinity groups, processing Whiteness, where often, I mean over 90 percent of the time, I observe White men will be the first, second, even third speakers unless there is some intervention for those with more marginalized identities to lead. I have often been, and still can be, that White man who speaks first. Given this observation, I have made a personal intention to listen first as often as I am self-aware of my own voice.

In doing this, I have found I am much quieter in meetings, and while teaching than in years past, I have also frequently found thoughts I might have shared are shared by others first, often negating my need to speak at all and reinforcing that I am not the sole keeper of knowledge and understanding in the universe. In staying quieter, I have realized so much of my desire to answer questions *first* and share my perspective *first* stems in large part from my ego and often serves to reinforce my privileged status. However, while I strive to listen first, listening first does not mean I stay quiet in the face of injustice. It is everyone's responsibility to speak out and act to confront all forms of injustice.

Now listening more in meetings or class is one thing, but keeping quiet in a room full of strangers in a session led by an icon is another.

I frequently choose to keep quiet as an excuse to avoid unease, discomfort, or vulnerability. I find it very easy to remain quiet in a space full of strangers who may publicly call me out on my blind spots as I share my faults. As I attempt to move beyond binaries, I try to accept the contradictory complex nature of this world and the idea that my staying quiet in this situation might simultaneously serve both justice and fear.

I believe there are many reasons I chose to stay quiet when Glenn Singleton asked, "Does anyone have any real breakthroughs they are having at this moment to share with the group?" But I wonder if I should have shared?

So, what was my breakthrough?

I found myself watching a historical video of LBJ in congress with two White men behind him and a sea of White men in front of him, and I started thinking, *While things are different today in Congress, they aren't that different.* At that moment, I checked in with my belief that racial equity benefits from White people stepping back from the often-limited seats of power and influence in the US; just as gender equity benefits from men stepping back from the often-limited seats of power and influence in the US. I believe these actions, especially for White men, support redistribution of access to positions of power, as clearly evidenced in Congress back in the 1960s and today.

I then personalized these thoughts, *As a White cisgender man, my actions over the past ten years in education have seen me climbing the pyramid, getting cushier chairs, and taking up more space at the table.* Most recently, I took a leadership role at a small education nonprofit organization with an all-White leadership team. It was an organization I knew would benefit from more BIPOC in leadership positions, yet I still took the most-recent available leadership role, a position I was able to secure through my various privileges, including privileged contacts and network.

When I think about the dissonance between my actions and what I want my beliefs to be, I usually try to avoid the natural feelings of discomfort that arise... *Maybe my deepest beliefs are not as egalitarian as I would like to think, maybe social justice is great as long as it does not affect my ability to live the life I want to live, maybe I am harboring a lot more racialized prejudice in my body and actions than I thought...* When my mind travels down these paths, I have so often chosen to close my heart off and say, "No, no, no just ignore, and these feelings will pass, just ignore, intellectualize, and these feelings will pass." But one of my biggest intentions lately has been to lean into my embodied feelings, and if I can't do it in a session aimed at getting us to do just that, I am in real trouble.

So, during the session, rather than step away from the discomfort in the dissonance between what I want my beliefs to be and my actual actions and merely step back and intellectualize what I was thinking as I tend to do (I *think* in large part because of my Whiteness and the comfort and praise I find in intellectualizing topics instead of embodying them), I leaned into the discomfort and unease bubbling in my stomach. Ironically, in addition to the discomfort, I also found myself feeling good just to be in my feelings.

After this, I mentally checked back in with the complex web of my beliefs and continued walking a circle of understanding from my beliefs to my thoughts to my feelings of discomfort. And I *thought* my justification (however flimsy) for taking my new job in management (at an organization I knew would benefit from BIPOC in leadership) was that if I had not taken it, the track record shows another White person probably would have—but we will never know. I should feel uneasy about that. I should feel discomfort around such actions. And this led me to the action (spurred by feelings of discomfort and hope) that at the very least, by taking this role I have a responsibility to push the organization to have a racial equity vision that will hopefully support more BIPOC on the board of directors and in leadership roles, I can also help push the organization to listen, center, and follow collective BIPOC voices.

After this circular process, there was still no closure, I still felt lots of discomfort with myself, *and* I felt centered. I felt a release of tension in my body and lungs as the feeling of being centered washed over me sitting, feet planting, backside against a particularly uncomfortable hotel conference chair.

Feeling centered was a breakthrough for me, a breakthrough I think I was able to achieve because I leaned into my feelings of discomfort, I strived to partially uncover my complex web of beliefs, I personalized my understanding of racial equity, and I connected all of this to actions for social justice. While I still have a long way to go, I still *feel* lots of discomfort. It *feels* good to begin to understand racial equity through personal reflection, beliefs, the feelings present in my body, and my actions simultaneously.

The Depth of Understanding

It is one thing to know theory. There is currently a large body of critical theory on the workings of White-supremacist thought, patriarchy, and exploitative capitalism to name a few. But simply knowing theory does not translate into reorienting mindsets, redistributing resources and opportunities, or building new interpersonal connections. In other words, simply knowing theory does not necessarily lead to social justice. To *understand* this body of work we must apply our critical theories to our daily lives and personal experiences (hooks, 2003).

Let's jump back for a second and ponder what *understanding* actually implies. As laid out in *UbD* (Wiggins & McTighe, 2008), *understanding* is the ability to transfer information in new contexts. This is more than knowledge; it is deeper because it requires transfer.

Knowledge is facts, information; while understanding is the ability to use that information and reconceptualize it. The authors of *UbD* provide the example that decoding and defining all the words in a given book is *knowledge*, while uncovering the theme of the book is *understanding*. If we take this idea of transferring knowledge and skills into the realm of social justice, understanding for social justice means being able to *transfer* knowledge into crushing cages (oppressive systems) and building nests (a brighter future). Using the preceding book analogy, understanding a text for social justice might mean applying the book's theme to our personal lives, using it to recognize and potentially shift our beliefs, acknowledging and accept the feelings that arise in our bodies as we read, or using it to instruct actions that support social justice.

For a more concrete example, it is one thing to define what racism is: "power + oppression = racism"—this is knowledge one can gain in a moment's search on Google. It is a whole different matter to *understand* that our personal identities wrapped in the intersection of race impacts our life chances and opportunities—this is transferring our knowledge into personalized understandings of racism. As we personalize our understanding of racism, we open the opportunity to recognize, confront, and potentially shift our beliefs. Diving deeper, because of our different lived experiences, we may all *feel* racism differently. As a White man, I will never have the embodied understanding of racism that a BIPOC individual may have in the US; however, I can still understand my own embodiment of racism or more aptly White privilege that relies on racism. When we are able to understand racism via our personalized experiences, beliefs, and embodiment, we are better situated to carry out meaningful anti-racist work, that is, actions.

However, action should not be viewed as the ultimate goal of understanding for social justice but rather one of multiple goals. Let's examine two common practices or *actions* in the sphere of social justice to illuminate this:

Limiting the use of the term *guys*: It is one thing to know that using the term *guys* to refer to any group of people regardless of gender status supports patriarchal thinking. After learning this, if one chooses, they can usually transfer this knowledge to stop saying "guys" when referring to individuals who do not identify as male in a matter of months. However, if one stops there, stops at this action, and does not dive deeper into understanding patriarchy and its many intersecting manifestations in one's personal experiences, beliefs and embodiment—deep understandings for social justice along with other meaningful actions—may be lost.

Providing gender pronouns at the end of an email: It is one thing to know that by adding their gender pronouns to their email signature signals an inclusive environment where people do not take the privilege of a singular, visible binary gender for grant it. This is knowledge that can lead to the action of creating a more inclusive environment. But again, if one stops here without an analysis of their personalized experiences, beliefs and honest feelings regarding the oppressive nature of gender normativity for individuals with nonbinary gender identities, a deep understanding for social justice along with other meaningful inclusive actions may be lost.

Let's review one more example: It's one thing to be able to define racial equity as a redistribution of access to resources and opportunities based on race; this is knowledge one can gain in the opening chapters of this book. It is a whole different matter to transfer this knowledge into understanding how as educators our daily actions align or disalign to redistributing resources and opportunities from White people toward BIPOC. Once we begin to personalize our understanding of racial equity, feelings naturally arise, and by leaning into those feelings, we can begin to tap into our complex web of beliefs and decide to pursue actions to disrupt the status quo.

Here we come back to intentions. Understanding for social justice requires us to go deeper than our actions, past personalizing knowledge to uncover and address our root intentions, our why. The actions of not using the term *guys* when referring to individuals who do not identify as guys, or listing your personal gender pronouns are positive actions for social justice. Actions for social justice are important, but so are being aware of our own experiences, our beliefs, and our embodied understandings. By transferring our knowledge of racism, patriarchy, gender biases, or any other oppressive systems to our personalized experiences, acknowledging and accepting our feelings and what is happening in our bodies, questioning our underlying beliefs, and pushing us to action altogether gets us closer to deep *understandings for social justice*.

Understanding for Social Justice

When I started speaking to colleagues about writing curriculum for social justice, I heard many of them say, "If the goal is action, then our understandings need to be about action." In understanding for social justice, we need to move beyond binaries toward both/and thinking. Understanding for social justice encapsulates both action and something more. If we jump toward action without really looking at our underlying truths and intentions, it is too easy for our actions to be swept away by the ever-rising tides of the status quo and a two-track educational system. Similarly, we can't just ask our students to jump toward action without analyzing their underlying truths and intentions. Understanding for social justice needs *both* action *and* something more. But what specifically is that *something more*?

There are several working theories and models related to "understanding for social justice." Some of the most impactful models that I have come across come from (a) Teaching for Tolerance, (b) Head, Heart, and Hands Model for Transformative Learning, and (c) Courageous Conversations.

Teaching for Tolerance

Teaching for Tolerance is an educational nonprofit offshoot of the Southern Poverty Law Center, and it provides a wealth of FREE resources to educators to inform their practices and to create civil and inclusive school communities where children are respected, valued, and welcome participants. Teaching for Tolerance divides teaching for social justice into four domains: Identity, Diversity, Justice, and Action. The Identity domain encapsulates developing positive social identities based on their membership in multiple groups in society. The Diversity domain encapsulates finding comfort with people who are both similar to and different and examines diversity in complex social, cultural, political, and historical contexts. The Justice domain encapsulates scholars recognizing that power and privilege influence relationships on interpersonal, intergroup, and institutional levels. The Action domain encapsulates students recognizing their own responsibility to stand up to exclusion, prejudice, and injustice and plan to carry out collective action against bias and injustice in the world. To address these domains, Teaching for Tolerance provides twenty age-appropriate anchor standards and learning outcomes to give educators common language and organizational structure to guide curriculum development.

Head, Heart, and Hands (HHH) Model for Transformative Learning

The HHH model was conceptualized from a synthesis of diverse literature, including sustainable education, transformative learning theories, Indigenous learning approaches, and experiential learning (Julie Singleton, 2015). This model is considered a holistic approach because it strives to teach to the whole human integrating learning across three domains: cognitive (head), affective (heart), and practical (hands) (Senka Gazibara, 2020). Proponents note that intentionally activating these three domains allows learners to fully engage in understanding. The head domain is most closely associated with examining biases and nurturing cultural competence. The heart domain connects to the transformational learning theory, which finds that scholars truly change mindsets when presented with whole-body experiences that shake their world perspective from the status quo into new learning in a manner that can be emotionally disorienting until the new learning is assimilated into a new understanding of the work and culture they are experiencing. The hand domain is about action and psychomotor engagement (Rhodes & Milby, 2016).

Courageous Conversations

Courageous Conversations (CC) is a tested protocol for effectively engaging, sustaining, and deepening interracial dialogue, initially conceived by Glenn Singleton over thirty years ago (Singleton, 2015). Within this protocol, one needs to take into account four different domains for how people process and understand issues surrounding race: (1) thinking, (2) believing, (3) feeling, and (4) doing. In this framework, one

> finds their center and potential understanding when they are able to navigate and balance all four ways of processing simultaneously. While conceived for processing issues surrounding race, I believe we can use the CC processing framework as a basis for building deep understandings for any social justice issue, as long we are viewing the issue via an intersectional lens that by definition takes into account race. Using the CC processing framework, one is on the path toward understanding for social justice when one is able to (1) get critical and personalize information; (2) recognize and potentially shift their beliefs; (3) recognize, accept, and use their feelings; and (4) create actions oriented toward social justice.

After reading how each of the above practices can inform understanding for social justice, notice how each underscores the importance of personal reflection, emotional intelligence, and the potential to incorporate somatics whether they label it identity, heart, or believing and feeling. Notice that each can align with critical pedagogy whether they label it diversity and justice, head, or thinking. Also notice that each of these models underscores the importance of action whether they label it action, hand, or doing.

A recurring theme throughout this book is not to dictate a single right approach in the face of all the other wrong approaches. Each of these models provides utility in constructing your own understandings for social justice related to your courses.

I personally lean toward the CC processing framework—you may have gleaned this preference throughout this book. I think I lean toward this framework because I like the clear language, separation of beliefs from feelings, and possibly because I was introduced to it before the other two models, or the idea that I feel a personal connection to Glenn Singleton, even though we have only briefly met. However, that is not to say this is the right framework and the others are wrong. For the detailed oriented individual who likes concrete examples, Teaching for Tolerance's four domains and twenty anchor standards with specified learning outcomes might be a great fit. For the individual who enjoys reviewing an extensive research base to believe in a practice, the HHH model has an extensive research base and may be a great fit for you.

When conceived using any of these frameworks, understanding for social justice is not about knowing the right or wrong answer, but it is a matter of degree on numerous domains, each with its own continuum that ranges from simple or superficial to complex and in-depth understandings.

Teaching understanding for social justice means we want our scholars to reach deep understandings: deep critical thinking, deep personal reflection, deep introspection, all leading toward meaningful actions.

So how do we get here? Review chapter 11: We backward design our curriculum from essential questions and deep enduring understandings for social justice that require students to meet grade-level standards along the way.

Essential Questions and Enduring Understandings

Essential questions (EQs) are really big open-ended questions that may be revisited over several years. Enduring understandings (EUs) are the other side of EQs; they are personalized, deep understandings that scholars develop and grow from working to address EQs. There are entire books written on how to construct EQs and EUs. I recommend reading *Essential Questions: Opening Doors to Student Understanding* (McTighe & Wiggins, 2013), and *Understanding by Design* (Wiggins & McTighe, 2008) to better understand each. In the rest of this chapter, I work to briefly summarize the collected works in this area, with added nuances to directly steer this work toward social justice.

Essential Questions (EQs) for Social Justice

For questions to be considered EQs, they should:

1. Be open-ended
2. Be thought-provoking, requiring higher-order thinking vs. simple recall
3. Be able to be revisited again and again
4. Be relevant
5. Be able to lead toward dismantling cages (systems of oppression) or building nests (a brighter interconnected future)

Taking a closer look at criteria #1, many questions can be "open-ended": How does oppression relate to our current global economic systems? How has science been used as a tool of oppression? How can artists use their mediums for social justice? On the other hand, some questions relevant to dismantling cages and building nests should *not* be open-ended. Even if we teach skills and content in a real-world context, but present that context from an "objective" or "neutral" perspective, we are supporting domination. As discussed in chapter 5, remaining neutral or pretending that objectivity is real is to side with the status quo and oppression. Our EQs cannot remain neutral; they must support students to take a stance for social justice.

EQs for social justice should not easily open the door for oppression and domination or allow us or our students to step back and take a neutral perspective. Let's look at some examples:

"Should statistics be used to oppress?" is not an appropriate EQ for social justice. Statistics should *never* be used to oppress. "*How* have statistics been used as a tool of domination," might be an EQ oriented toward social justice. An even stronger question that opens the door to positive framing might be, "How *can* statistics be used as a tool of *both* domination and social justice?"

"Should we incarcerate more Black and Brown people than White people per capita?" is not an EQ for social justice. We should not. "*How* has US history over the past three hundred years led to the mass incarceration of Black and Brown people in the US?" might be an EQ oriented toward social justice, although a stronger EQ might be, "How can we dismantle generationally oppressive systems that have led to the mass incarceration of Black and Brown folks?"

"Is it okay for the US government to break its treaty with Native peoples to run the Dakota Access Pipeline through Standing Rock Sioux tribal land?" is not an EQ for social justice. It is not *okay*. "How can ecology be used to bolster protesting oppressive government decisions?" might be an EQ oriented toward social justice. If we accept the essential question, "Is it okay for the US government to break its treaty with Native peoples to run the Dakota Access Pipeline through Standing Rock Sioux tribal land?" we could lead our students to the enduring understanding that it is okay to oppress Native Peoples in support of the exploitative capitalist marketplace and the colonization of "other" people's land that exploitative capitalism breeds. In many cases, our EQs cannot be objective[41] because they must lead to enduring understandings that dismantle cages and build nests.

Going back to take a closer look at other points from our criteria for EQs for social justice, let's look at criteria #3: EQs should be able to be revisited again and again. They can be either overarching and revisited year after year, or more topical and revisited over just a few lessons.

Both criteria #4 (EQs should be relevant) and #5 (EQs should lead toward dismantling cages or building nests) require that EQs

---

[41] See page 86-87 for a description of issues with objectivity.

relate to the context of your students. Here we come back to *relevance* as addressed in chapter 9 and *authenticity* as addressed in chapter 5. When knowing if an EQ is relevant to our students, we need to ask: Is this question in the important interest of my learners' understanding? We cannot answer this in isolation. To answer this, we must work with our students, their families, and their communities, especially when they differ from our own.

Enduring Understandings (EUs) for Social Justice

Our EUs for social justice are more than knowledge, they are the other side of EQs. They are the higher-order thinking and the transferable ideas that EQs lead us toward in order to dismantle cages and build nests. EUs for social justice must require scholars to do the work inherent in our domains of understanding for social justice: thinking, believing, feeling, and doing (or whatever domain names you choose to use). Additionally, because curriculum writing for social justice requires rigorous demands (see chapter 9), EUs for social justice should require students demonstrate understanding of grade-level standards while doing the work. Ultimately, the work of EUs for social justice should lead scholars to personalize knowledge, uncover and potentially shift beliefs, recognize, invoke, acknowledge, and/or use embodied feelings, and lead toward action all while meeting grade-level standards along the path.

Revisiting some of our examples of EQs oriented toward social justice above, we can combine each with potential EUs that open the doors to critical thinking and deep personal reflection, leading toward meaningful actions while requiring students meet grade-level rigor:

EQ: How can statistics be used as a tool of both domination and social justice?

EU: Statistics are not inherently biased, but people's conscious and unconscious interpretations and use of statistics often are; people can both wield statistics for oppressive purposes, disguising it as fact, and for social justice.

To meet the preceding goals, EU scholars could be required to apply their understanding of grade-level standards related to statistics to be critical thinkers, address how manipulating statistics makes them feel, discuss statistics that question their beliefs, and use statistics to inspire action that deconstructs cages and builds nests.

EQ: How can we dismantle generationally oppressive systems that have led to the mass incarceration of Black and Brown folks?

EU: Students will understand how the historical context (over the past four hundred years) for the mass incarceration of Black and Brown folks in the US relates to their personal experience and power.

To meet the preceding goal, EU scholars could be required to meet grade-level standards in social studies and/or common core reading standards. Curriculum related to this understanding could open the door to critical thinking, personal reflection, feelings, shifting beliefs, and inspire action that deconstructs cages and builds nests.

Notice that both of these examples *could* be used for specific subjects (math and social studies, respectively), but each also maintains the potential for interdisciplinarity (*Beyond Binaries and Borders* chapters 5 and 8). Also notice that I frequently use the qualifier *could*... Each of the preceding EUs *could* lead to students meeting grade-level standards; critical thinking; personal reflection; recognizing, invoking, acknowledging, and/or shifting embodied beliefs and feelings; or motivating action. EQs and EUs do not necessarily lead to any of these goals on their own. It is through our *assessments* that we begin to bring our EUs and EQs to life and begin to meet their complex intentions for curriculum oriented toward social justice.

Recap and Moving Forward

Given what we have covered on essential questions, we should remember that by definition there is not a single right answer for this chapter's essential questions: What is the difference between knowing and understanding? What is the connection between transfer and social justice?

Ideally, this chapter has sparked you to understand that we need complex enduring understandings that provide an opportunity to intertwine rigorous grade-level skills with social justice content in hopes that what we teach students can be transferred into social justice. However, as Wiggins and McTighe (2008) note, "No question is inherently essential or trivial. Whether it is essential depends on purpose, audience, context, and impact." So, too, no question or understanding for social justice can in itself lead to social justice. This hinges on purpose, audience, context, and impact.

It is through our assessments that we begin to bring our EQs and EUs oriented toward social justice to life—ideally so our questions and understandings support grade-level rigor while leading scholars to (1) critically analyze and personalize information; (2) recognize and potentially shift personal embodied beliefs; (3) acknowledge, accept, invoke, and potentially alter personal embodied feelings; and/or (4) lead scholars to take actions that deconstruct cages and/or build nests for social justice.

# Chapter 13

Assessment for Social Justice

Standardized exams drive everything from curriculum to teaching. As a result, many teachers believe that anything aside from teaching to the test will be detrimental to students and teachers alike...Teachers become adept at creating high-pressure classrooms focused more on testing than teaching. Teachers are reduced to test-prep machines. White folks who teach in the hood are particularly prone to this sort of rote model. This is especially the case if they are convinced that having all students pass tests creates some form of equity. In these cases they are so married to a curriculum that is sold as the only path to passing the test that there is no willingness to deviate from it even if it is harming students. Furthermore, teaching to an exam and strictly following a curriculum makes it easier for these teachers to remain emotionally disconnected from students.

— Dr. Emdin (2017), self-identifies as a Black man

Essential Guiding Question: How can assessment allow students to demonstrate understandings for social justice and aid in dismantling cages and/or building nests, without reducing teaching to high-pressure test prep?

Narrative: Mr. Sternstein

Mr. Sternstein was the first teacher to give me an A. In fact, he was the only teacher to give me an A in high school outside of an art class. Prior to Mr. Sternstein, my report cards were filled with Ds and Cs and comments like, "I know he understands the material, if he just completed the work he would get a good grade," or "If Ian would just try a little harder, I think he could actually do well."

Mr. Sternstein was my 10th-, 11th-, and 12th-grade English teacher. He passed away during the COVID pandemic in New York City, but his teachings have stayed with me since 10th grade, and I know he will stay with me long after his passing.

Mr. Sternstein began every year by stating that merely doing *the work* would not get you an A in his class. His class was one of the hardest to get an A in. The only way to get an A was to demonstrate deep understandings as evidenced during class discussions, writing assignments, and projects.

He also didn't like to talk about grades. He refused to give one their grade when asked. And he refused to grade our assignments; instead, he gave us copious amounts of comments. He even refused to give a concrete definition for how to get an A in his class beyond informing us that after his many years of teaching, he innately *knew* what an A looks like in discussions and writing, or what a B looks like, and what a C looks like, and so on. He had been teaching for more than thirty years by the time I had him as my teacher. I can only imagine the complexities of the rubric he held in his head that he refused to share.

In Mr. Sternstein's English classes, every discussion was an assessment, every paper or project was an assessment, and assessments were never given a grade. We only knew what grade we were receiving in his class when he returned a paper.

He wrote his feedback comments in large, almost illegible cursive, scrawling across our pages when he returned a paper, but he wrote our grade for his class in the tiniest print in the upper left-hand corner of our papers.

The grade was not for the paper—the paper was filled with comments—that was our feedback for our writing, not a grade. The grade was what he thought we had earned in his class up to that point using his thirty-plus years of intuition and experience.

How did I get an A in Mr. Sternstein's classes when I failed in most other spaces? How is it that writing filled with grammar and spelling errors such as "human-beans," didn't hold me back? How did the classic signs of my Dyslexia and ADHD (spelling and grammar issues or failing to complete busy work outside of the classroom) not hinder my ability to excel in Mr. Sternstein's class?

As with most phenomena in life, there are a number of reasons from Mr. Sternstein's deep love of his subject and students to my personal privilege such as having the fortune to see an incredible tutor who helped me learn the mechanics of reading and writing while in high school. But in particular, I think Mr. Sternstein's focus on deep understandings over busy work played a large role.

We never had a multiple-choice assessment in Mr. Sternstein's class. We never had lectures. We never sat in silent rows. Class was set up in a circle. We had discussions. We worked in groups and received huge amounts of feedback. Mr. Sternstein's room was a room filled with learning, not busy work. There was no sage on the stage who had all the answers; there was nothing to memorize.

Mr. Sternstein lived by the mantra: "Look at the fish." This was taken from a story where a student was told to write down everything she could observe regarding a dead fish. After completing her list, her teacher told her to find more and write more. After completing a second list, her teacher told her to find more ---> maybe you see where this is going. There is always more depth to be discovered. We can always stand to look longer at the fish.

Mr. Sternstein's assessments were about pushing our depth of thinking while making it all visible for meaningful feedback and pushes.

Assessment is a fish I have strived to understand, a fish I have worked to look closer at—one I know still needs more study.

Assessment Is Not a Dirty Word

In my first year student teaching at a restrictive Level IV facility for students with behavioral difficulties deemed too severe to be in a normal school building, I remember walking into class one morning and stating, in a sarcastic and joking tone, "Pop quiz!" I was not serious; we literally never had any quizzes. However, my students did not pick up on the dry wit and rapidly began screaming obscenities and flipping tables in fear, anger, and disgust.

I did not make a "joke" like that again.

While my students' reactions to the word *quiz* was extreme, I see the glints of similar disgust, anger, or fear whenever I mention the word *assessment*, whether to other educators, pre-service teachers, or students.

But assessment does not need to be a dirty, scary, or anger-invoking word. The intentions behind our assessments dictate the degree to which an assessment will be oppressive or liberating, not the idea of assessment.

Throughout this book, we have reviewed the importance of intentions in orienting any work toward social justice. Intentionality continues to be a key when designing meaningful assessments for curriculum oriented toward social justice.

There are countless intentions behind assessing students: to gauge how we instructed; to inform future instructional decisions; to provide an easy activity for a sub covering our class; to fulfill a mandatory category in our gradebook; to comply with mandated state or district testing; to tell ourselves we are preparing students for mandated state or district testing; to apply for various federal and state title funds; or to inflict punishment to name just a few. There are meaningful reasons to assess students just as there are oppressive reasons too. In and of itself, *assessment* is neither oppressive nor liberating; how and why we assess can be either and both.

What Is the Purpose of Assessment for Understanding?

In a classroom focused on building deep understandings, a foundational reason to assess is to collect evidence of student understanding. Remember that understanding requires transferring or applying knowledge or skills in novel situations; therefore, evidence of understanding means we need performance evidence not evidence of memorization (whether memorization of facts or skills). The authors of *UbD* (McTighe & Wiggins, 2008) pose the following questions to ascertain if an assessment requires performance:

Does the assessment amount to just a simplified 'drill' out of context? Or does the assessment require students to really 'perform' wisely with knowledge and skill, in a problematic context of real issues, needs, constraints, and opportunities?

To connect evidence of understanding directly to social justice, our problematic context of real issues, needs, constraints, and opportunities must align with social justice; it must align with tasks that support understandings for social justice (as discussed in chapter 12), while students demonstrate the transfer of grade-level standards.

Ron Ritchhart (2015), who identifies as growing up in rural Indiana, attending public school, and teaching for fourteen years before becoming a researcher, argues in *Creating Cultures of Thinking* that the best performance tasks are deep, as compared to surface level. Surface-level tasks focus on memorization, whereas deep tasks focus on developing enduring understandings with transfer and application. Think of surface-level tasks as leading toward *reproduction*, and deep tasks as leading toward *construction*. When I think about these words, curriculums oriented toward social justice should not be about *reproducing* the status quo and a two-track oppressive educational system but *constructing* something new and beautiful. Therefore, as we are designing our evidence of understanding, we should include deep performance tasks that intertwine grade-level skills with relevant understandings for social justice.

To build ever deeper understandings, scholars need a sequence of authentic, novel performance tasks increasing in complexity over time with constant feedback on performance. In this way, assessments for understanding are more like a scrapbook of learnings over time than a single snapshot (McTighe & Wiggins, 2008).

While these frequent tasks increase in complexity, they should always require students to demonstrate the ability to "do" grade-level standards to complete, as well as address understanding for social justice.

How to Orient Assessments Toward Social Justice

For an assessment to orient toward social justice in the *Justice by Design* framework it should:

- ❖ Support building nests, and/or crushing cages.
- ❖ Support scholars to transfer knowledge and/or skills into understandings for social justice that require scholars to (1) critically analyze and personalize information; (2) recognize and potentially shift personal embodied beliefs; (3) recognize, invoke, accept, and/or potentially alter personal embodied feelings; and/or (4) lead scholars to take actions oriented toward social justice.
- ❖ Require scholars to meet the depth of grade-level rigor (standards) to complete

In creating assessments that collect evidence of understanding for social justice in this way, I find it is helpful to think of big assessments and little assessments.

Big assessments are completed over several lessons, weeks, or even months, while little assessments might be completed in one lesson on a daily or weekly interval schedule. Big assessments are bigger in scope, potentially covering several standards and understandings for social justice. Little assessments are smaller in scope covering fewer standards and most likely only a piece of understanding for social justice. To use the scrapbook metaphor, big assessments might be the scrapbook, while little assessments are the individual moments in the scrapbook. By nature, big assessments may be more summative[42] than little assessments, but both forms should provide opportunities for feedback, making them both formative[43]. I am of the belief all assessments should be used in a formative capacity to some degree.

In planning what such assessments for social justice might look like, we find the perfect place to begin inserting our pedagogies oriented toward social justice. Big and little assessments may both include:

- Critical literacy questions
- Self-reflective questions
- Storytelling for social justice
- Artistically expressive projects
- Action-oriented research projects
- Somatic-based questions and role plays
- Cooperative learning assignments
- Questions or reflections in Circle discussions or cooperative groups

Examples of Assessments for Social Justice

---

[42] The general goal of summative assessment is to evaluate student learning at the end of an instructional unit.

[43] The general goal of formative assessment is to monitor student learning during an instructional unit to provide ongoing feedback that can be used by instructors to improve their teaching and by students to improve their learning.

Let's start by examining two small assessments that potentially fit into a class period along with the learning activities that might lead toward the assessments.

Class: 7th-Grade Math
Unit 1 Essential Question: How can we use algebraic principles to support action for social justice? **Unit 1 Enduring Understanding:** Math can be used to model intersectional oppressive systems providing evidence to change systems.
7th-Grade Math Standard Alignment: CCSS RP.A.3 "Use proportional relationships to solve multistep ratio and percent problems." (e.g., simple interest)
Small Assessment Tasks
Letter to a Legislator: Write a letter to your local state legislator, mayor, or governor asking them to draft legislation that minimizes intersectional race/gender bias in housing loan interest rates. In your letter, you must provide justification for your request using a mathematical simple interest model with real-world data. For your mathematical model, use the median home value in your neighborhood, city, or state. **Closing Reflection Questions:** How did this data make you feel? How can understanding algebra help us take action for social justice? What other actions can you take in the face of the injustices described today?
Classroom Activities (leading toward the small assessments): **As a class:** The teacher presents the simple interest equation* to students and describes each variable in the equation. Then the teacher describes what a mortgage rate is and how total payments are calculated using a mortgage rate with the simple interest equation.

In Pairs: Students answer the following questions while the teacher circulates supporting groups as they learn how to transfer mathematical terms from the word problem below into the simple interest equation and then solve.

- **Background:** On average, White men in America pay 7.1% mortgage rates, while Black women pay 7.9%**

- **Problem:** Given these different mortgage rates, after a thirty-year, fixed loan, how much will a White man pay for a $100,000 house? How much will a Black woman pay?

- **Critical Thinking Questions:** What implications does this intersectional race/sex difference have? How does this relate to White privilege? (*Intersectionality* and *White privilege* are terms that would have been reviewed in a prior class)

Individual: Once pairs demonstrate understanding on their questions above, the teacher gives them the *Letter to a Legislator* assessment to complete independently.

Teachers should be prepared as needed to describe what a mathematical model is to students; where to find who their state legislator, mayor, and governor are; and where to find the median home value in their chosen area.

Closing: After completing the letter assessment, students complete the reflection questions either as homework or in a Circle discussion format in class if there is time.

Prerequisites: Students are familiar with the terms *White privilege* and *intersectionality*. Students are familiar with partner work. Students are familiar with how to construct mathematical models. Students are familiar with how to use online search engines with teacher guidance.

*$A=P(1+rt)$ | A=Final Amount; P=Initial Principal Balance; r=Annual Interest rate; t=Time in years

**data from www.MotherJones.com

> **Potential**: The Letter assessment has the potential to support students in transferring grade level rigor (i.e., The *percent* aspect of CCSS RP.A.3) into an action related to social justice. This captures the idea that understanding for social justice requires in part transferring knowledge and skills into action.
>
> The reflection questions assessment has the potential to allow students to address their feelings and beliefs related to an intersectional injustice, and showcase their brilliance in coming up with new ways of taking action.

Now let's take a look at a big assessment, along with a brief description of small assessments that both provide learning experiences and a scrapbook of visible thinking leading toward the big assessment.

Class: 9th-Grade English Language Arts
Unit 1 Essential Question: How can one find power in marginalized identities? **Unit 1 Enduring Understanding:** Scholars will understand personal and societal relationships between identity and power.
Big Assessment Task: At the end of Unit 1, scholars must write a "superhero" story where their superhero's powers are derived from a characteristic of the author that has been marginalized in our society (identity domains that may be marginalized: weight, skin color, hair texture, age, disability status, etc.) and is used to fight some form of intersectional injustice. The story must meet grade-level writing standards for narrative storytelling. Peers will peer review each other's stories and provide meaningful feedback.
Standards Addressed During Unit 1:

CCSS.ELA-LITERACY.W.9-10.3.B: Use narrative techniques, such as dialogue, pacing, description, reflection, and multiple plot lines, to develop experiences, events, and/or characters

CCSS.ELA-LITERACY.RI.9-10.4: Determine the meaning of words and phrases as they are used in a text, including figurative, connotative, and technical meanings; analyze the cumulative impact of specific word choices on meaning and tone (e.g., how the language of a court opinion differs from that of a newspaper).

CCSS.ELA-LITERACY.RI.9-10.5: Analyze in detail how an author's ideas or claims are developed and refined by particular sentences, paragraphs, or larger portions of a text (e.g., a section or chapter).

CCSS.ELA-LITERACY.RI.9-10.6: Determine an author's point of view or purpose in a text and analyze how an author uses rhetoric to advance that point of view or purpose.

VA:Cr1.2.IIa: Choose from a range of materials and methods of traditional and contemporary artistic practices to plan works of art and design.

Small Assessments Throughout Unit 1 Building Toward the Big Assessment:

- ❖ Scholars complete five readings on the topic of marginalization and answer text-dependent[44] critical literacy questions and self-reflection questions to better understand the concept of marginalization.

- ❖ Scholars read three excerpts from stories containing characters marginalized in society who find self-empowerment and answer text-dependent critical literacy questions and self-reflection questions to better understand the concept of marginalization.

- ❖ Readings, questions, and written responses all align to grade-level ELA standards (See list above)

---

[44] Questions that can only be answered by referring explicitly back to the text being read.

> ❖ Scholars will have four opportunities to practice writing grade-level narrative writing skills aligned with grade-level ELA standard 9-10.3.B via writing prompts prior to their big assessment.
>
> Scholars will create a cover image using a visual medium to add to their narrative story for social justice aligned to VA:Cr1.2.IIa (see above)

> **Potential:** Between both the big and small assessment tasks there is the potential to:
>
> Foster deep understandings for social justice via personalizing understandings of marginalization and empowerment, evoking feelings through the process of storytelling, and change beliefs by reading peers' stories.
>
> Deconstruct cages by imagining how to fight a form of intersectional injustice.
>
> Build nests by imagining how to find power in a marginalized identity characteristic.
>
> Demonstrate understanding of grade-level standards.

In the preceding examples, the possibilities of small assessments and classroom activities really are endless, and will of course need endless revisions and iterations whatever they are. Additionally, as with any instruction, how these assessments and activities are ultimately brought to life can vary dramatically depending on where an individual teacher, and individual students are at in their personal journeys and understandings of algebra, writing, reading comprehension, and social-justice-oriented mindsets. Also, notice my biases in presenting these two assessments, both of which lean heavily on writing. I definitely have a bias toward incorporating the written word into assessments. My use of two such examples here should not be taken as writing is the best, most rigorous or most meaningful form of assessment; valuable assessments come in many different forms.

Whatever big and little assessments one chooses to design, using our backward design process, the final products must align to our deep enduring understandings and essential questions oriented toward social justice while intertwining grade-level rigor. To help students reach these deep and rigorous understandings, they will need consistent feedback along the path.

Feedback

Feedback is essential to growth. Complex assessments along with probing questions and observation can help to make student learning visible, which allows us to see what feedback may be most supportive to our scholar's growth. Ideally, the most-effective feedback is timely, descriptive, and task based.

To support student growth, our assessments and lesson plans need to create space for constant, timely, descriptive task-based feedback, which can come from teachers, peers, and self. Two keys to supporting effective feedback are (1) knowing the ultimate goals for instruction, and (2) recognizing the developmental range of understandings leading to our ultimate goals. Once we understand the developmental range, we can better predict where misconceptions might lie and how to intervene for students anywhere on the continuum of understanding.

Side note: grades/scores are a form of feedback; however, research has demonstrated that grades are not an effective form of feedback because they can actually interfere with student learning. Oftentimes, students with high grades/scores can view feedback as unnecessary, while students with low grades/scores can view feedback as undesirable. Additionally, the strongest feedback focuses on the learning not the learner—grades tend to focus on the learner, while descriptive feedback focuses more on the learning (Erkens & Schimmer, 2017). This is not to say grades are evil, and descriptive feedback is good. Again, we need to move beyond binaries. Grades have the potential and power to showcase, value, and celebrate student brilliance. However, we should not think of grades as a form of feedback and we should find ways to ensure grading does not interfere with student growth.[45]

While grading can be counterproductive to learning at times, we still need a way to measure student growth and understanding on our messy real-world tasks. We still need a way to make our expectations for an assessment concrete. Rubrics support us to this end, that is unless one has tens of years of experience and can hold complex rubrics in their head like Mr. Sternstein in my

---

[45] Read *Grading for Equity* by Joe Feldman (2018) for some great ideas on how to accomplish this.

opening narrative (though I do think a rubric may have been very useful to me as a student in his class).

Rubrics

Crucial questions for messy real-world application tasks include: How do we measure growth and depth? How do we streamline feedback? How do we support our learners in focusing their work? We can accomplish these *hows* by creating rubrics for our assessments. Because understanding for social justice is a complex matter of degree on numerous continuums and not about getting answers simply right or wrong, evaluation of student work needs to be able to address these complexities with concrete criteria. A rubric for understanding can provide concrete criteria for articulating what understanding for social justice might look like on your given assessment, and what separates more superficial and simplistic responses from deeper and complex responses.

There is a wealth of resources for constructing rubrics out there. Rather than recreate these resources here, I would add that our rubrics ultimately define what we think is important in a given assessment task. For example, if we think demonstrating the transfer of a particular grade-level standard is important to our assessment task, we should have lines devoted to this in our rubric. If we think working collaboratively as a group is important, we should have lines in our rubric devoted to group work or group leadership skills. If we think self-reflection and somatics are important to our assessment task, we should have lines devoted to this in our rubric. If we think taking real-world concrete actions for social justice is important to our assessment task, we should have lines devoted to this in our rubric.

When creating a rubric, every line item should have a set of descriptors ranging from simple/superficial understandings of the desired item to complex/deep understandings of the desired item. For example, a rubric for the superhero story assessment above for a 9th-grade social studies class might include:

Superhero Assignment Rubric			
Score Continuum	**1 pt**	**3 pts**	**5 pts**
Meets Grade-Level Standard: CCSS.ELA-LITERACY.W.9-10.3.B (Use narrative techniques, such as dialogue, pacing, description, reflection, and multiple plot lines to develop experiences, events, and/or characters)	**Novice** Can perform this standard only with coaching or highly scripted writing organizers.	**Able** Limited but growing ability to be adaptive in executing this standard. May be masterful in some but not all aspects of this standard, or may be only okay in transferring all aspects of this standard.	**Masterful** Fluent and flexible ability to transfer all skills related to this standard into narrative writing.
Narrative Conveys Powerful Self-Reflection	**Naive** Narrative does not portray an understanding of personal power, privileged identities, or	**Reflective** Narrative portrays a partial understanding of personal power, privileged	**Insightful** Narrative clearly portrays a deep understanding of personal power, privileged

	marginalized identities.	identities, and/or marginalized identities.	identities, and/or marginalized identities.
Narrative Contains Meaningful Use of Metaphors	**Absent** The narrative does not include any *meaningful* metaphors for oppression and social justice.	**Present** The narrative contains metaphors for oppression and social justice, but metaphors are not central to the theme.	**Wise** The narrative contains one or more metaphors that are central to the story's theme and that relate to oppression and social justice.
Accurate Presentation: Including Formatting (font, size, spacing, subheadings, etc.), Grammar, Punctuation, and Spelling	**Poor** Issues with formatting, grammar, punctuation, and/or spelling make it difficult to fluently read and follow the narrative.	**Okay** There are some issues with either formatting, grammar, punctuation, or spelling, but these issues do not interfere greatly with fluently reading and following the narrative.	**Strong** Format makes it easy to read and follow. Grammar, spelling, and punctuation support readability and are accurate for their desired goal within the context of the narrative.
Cover Art Meets Grade-Level Art Standard: VA:Cr1.2.IIa (Choose from a range of materials and methods of traditional and contemporary artistic practices to plan works of art and design.)	**Not Observed** Does not take into account a range of materials and methods of both traditional and contemporary artistic practices when planning a work in response to a new creative problem.	**Limited Evidence** Chooses from a limited range of materials and methods of traditional or contemporary artistic practices to plan a work in response to a	**Sufficient Evidence** Chooses from a range of materials and methods of traditional and contemporary artistic practices to plan a work in response to a new creative problem.

			new creative problem.	
Peer Review: Provide Feedback to Peer	**Independent** Did not review a peer's essay.	**Supportive** Read a peer's essay and provided global feedback (e.g., "Good job"), but not specific, effective feedback.	**Cooperative** Read a peer's essay and provided lots (10–20 comments) of specific effective feedback for peer's writing.

Notice that we can combine standards from multiple disciplines, creating an interdisciplinary assessment. Notice that we can intertwine criteria from grade-level standards and deeper understandings for social justice. Don't focus on the format, the headings, the number of criteria, the points associated with each criterion, or the depth written into a line of criteria (such as putting all of one standard into a single criterion, versus breaking the multiple skills present in each standard into several criteria across several rows); these are more superficial aspects that can be adapted to suit your design preferences.

The key takeaway is that rubrics can provide us with more specific criteria to make the degree of understanding captured on our assessments slightly more concrete, while also narrowing one's focus for a given assessment. This detail, in turn, gives us another window into what we must cover in our instruction leading up to the final assessment. For example, here it lets us know that we must cover: (1) all the skills present in standards CCSS.ELA-

LITERACY.W.9-10.3.B and VA:Cr1.2.IIa, (2) powerful self-reflection, (3) the use of meaningful metaphors, (4) presentation of writing, and (5) effective peer feedback—all in addition to the content we wish to cover regarding storytelling, marginalization, and empowerment. Creating rubrics like this helps to illustrate what will be needed throughout our unit, ensuring that our unit aligns well to the depth of this assessment. Note: when having difficulty formulating a rubric, or the criteria you wish to portray in a given assessment, it can be very helpful to create exemplar examples of your assessment.

Recap and Moving Forward

So how do we avoid Dr. Emdin's (2017) honest and apt critiques of turning classrooms into standardized test-prep rooms, especially in "the hood"? We create meaningful assessments that demonstrate understanding for social justice, provide space for feedback, and aid in dismantling cages or building nests. And we ensure our curriculums are backward designed to these meaningful assessments and not backward designed to standardized tests. In turn, when our meaningful assessments align with the transfer of rigorous standards intertwined with understanding for social justice, our students' scores on *those* standardized tests should increase as a side effect of good teaching. How do we accomplish this? We turn our carefully honed EQs and EUs for social justice into rigorous, messy, meaningful performance tasks.

Chapter 14

Putting It All Together

Half the curriculum walks in the door when the students do.

— EMILY STYLE (1988), SELF-IDENTIFIES AS A WHITE WOMAN.

Essential Question: What does *Justice by Design* mean to you?

Narrative: Writing *Justice by Design*

In writing this book, I went through a number of fears. The fear that I co-opted and appropriated the work of others, especially other BIPOC and women—to push a system shrouded in beautiful quotes by other writers yet could still be twisted to oppress. The fear that writing a book about teaching for social justice actually allows me to distance myself from the very students and communities I strive to support in social justice (be they White; Black; Brown; Indigenous; Asian; impoverished or wealthy; male, female, or nonbinary; documented or undocumented; disabled or not). I felt many of the fears inherent in an imposter complex writing this book:

> Who am I to write *Justice by Design*? What have I accomplished? I cannot say I have arrived. Even after all the settings I have taught in, I cannot say I ever truly realized the goals of *Justice by Design*. I have not personally

lived the vision of this book. If people were to observe many of my classrooms over my years teaching, I would embody the opportunity myth and a two-track system. I cannot say Justice by Design provides a tested three-step program guaranteed to bring about social justice every time. More so, what right does another White guy even have to talk about designing curriculum for social justice?

Believe me, I felt the *feels* inherent in the imposter complex writing this book—including guilt.

Guilt is an easy place to go, especially when one occupies identities and positions of power and privilege, like a cisgender White male program manager. In all my years in school I was culpable with hierarchical systems, with the opportunity myth and a two-track education system. For all my years in education, I was also fortunate to work in schools I love, with children and staff I love, doing work I love and have yet to reach the vision so many of my institutions promised our scholars and families. And I feel guilty that if I were better or just did a little bit more maybe I could have helped realize that vision sooner. What if I just spent a few more hours coaching teachers or writing curriculum or what if I personally fulfilled that homeschool assignment or what if…fill in the blank. One can always give more. But does giving more to assuage guilt, or to *play the hero*, actually lead to long-term justice?

The truth is feeling guilt is not productive. Feeling *lesser than* because we did not give even more does not lead to sustainability. Feeling shitty only wastes precious time or inevitably leads to making others feel shitty. Doing the work of *Justice by Design* is struggling with our failures and egos and choosing to adapt, change, and move toward the pleasure in justice rather than the pain of inadequacy. In the words of Adrienne Maree Brown (2017), "I choose what to embody, what to long for, even as the horizon shifts before me. The adaptation is up to me. The laughter between grieving friends, the justice of advancing a righteous anger, the first moments of surrender into new love, the opportunity inside of apparent failure… How often, how quickly can I become aware of the miraculous nature of the moment I am in, and adapt towards the pleasure available in that awareness?"

In writing this book, I went down the road of feeling self-failure and feeling inadequate and guilty. In these moments, I found the opportunity to read, reflect, talk, connect with loved ones, connect with new acquaintances, write, grow, adapt, and work on my personal practice. In the end, doing my self-work I came across Edgar Villanueva's (2018) writing on decolonizing philanthropy in the US. To repeat his words from the first chapter of this book: "For most people, medicine is something used to treat or cure a disease, often a man-made drug or sometimes an herb… In Native traditions, however, medicine is a way of achieving balance… And the practice of medicine is not just limited to the hands of medicine people: everyone is welcome to participate." Villanueva underscores the importance of discovering one's medicine. Through doing my self-work, I realized that writing—curriculum, blogs, podcasts, books—represents my medicine for healing from the virus of colonization.

Healing needs a starting point. Let's move past the barriers that may be hindering your personal progress and start together. For me, that means moving past fear, guilt, and doubt to action, to difficult self-work, to uncovering my true embodied beliefs and shifting them, to accepting my authentic feelings and finding more joy, to understanding my role in both oppressive and liberating systems. Knowing all the while that my actions will be imperfect. *Perfection is a tool of the oppressor.* We just need to start. Start and iterate. Start and connect with others. Start and find the pleasure and the joy and the hope in putting it all together for social justice.

Putting It All Together

In writing a curriculum oriented toward social justice, we need to be bold and do things differently. Doing things the same only ensures more of the same, more of the status quo, more of a two-track educational system, more inequity, more injustice by design. We need to be bold and do things differently.

Differently begins with self-work. Unapologetically uncovering our beliefs, accepting our feelings to make personal changes in our mindsets where we need to. While "differently" begins with self-work, it does not wait for us to figure out all our baggage before working to design curriculum oriented toward social justice for the students we will face tomorrow. Our students cannot wait for us.

We must move into the space of discomfort, knowing that our self-work is a never-ending process, and we must not wait to *understand it all* before attempting to teach, which means we will make mistakes. You will make mistakes. I have made and will continue to make mistakes. Mistakes that will cause pain and hurt and harm. Harm that we must repair through honest reflection, vulnerability, and open hearts.

Accept that despite all the intention we put into our practice we will still cause harm. Know the difference between intention and impact and that causing harm through your impact regardless of intention regardless of your why and your self-work does not make you evil, just human. Accept your imperfections. Acknowledge your impact, the good and bad. Be vulnerable. Listen. Feel.

We must reflect to acknowledge our harm, we must support a space where those who have been harmed can express the impact of that harm, and we must ask what the needs of those who have been harmed are. We must listen and act with an open loving heart that transforms personal shame into accountability and restorative justice, not defensiveness. We must be models of both victim and perpetrator in restorative justice, restoring humanity in ourselves and our classrooms. We must step out of the oppressive confines of perfection into the freedom of simply starting, knowing that if we love ourselves, we can find the resiliency needed to confront our mistakes, repair with those we will harm, and adapt.

Steps and Questions

Because questions are at the foundation of strong instruction, so too are questions at the foundation of meaningful instructional design. For those who enjoy steps and guiding questions as much as I do, here is how I put it all together to get started, knowing that due to the messy real world, this is not a linear process but an iterative one, especially given the numerous questions to consider at each step, the countless other questions we, or at least I, do not yet know to ask.

Step 1: Self-Work
Purpose
Why is your work for social justice personally important? What does social justice mean to you? What is your purpose and vision for designing curriculum oriented toward social justice? Are you prepared to let your understanding, purpose, and vision grow with the shifting horizon?
Love
What does real love mean to you? Do you truly take care of yourself? Do you respect yourself? Do you trust yourself and your intentions? Can you forgive yourself when you do not live up to your personal expectations? What place does love have in your classroom?
Your Book of Law
What are your actual intentions, beliefs, and feelings about teaching, about your students' potential, about your

potential—the good, the ugly, the contradictory? Have you honestly looked in the mirror to better know yourself and your *book of law*? How can you involve your whole being: mind, body, and soul, in understanding and realizing your beliefs, purpose, and vision for curriculum oriented toward social justice?

Your Students

Do you truly care about and feel empathy, including kinesthetic empathy[46], for your students? Do you really *know* your students, their families, their desires, their struggles? Do you always show your students culturally responsive[47] respect? Do you hold yourself and your students to high expectations? Do you trust *your* future to your students? What happens when you assume all of your students are brilliant?

Growth

Do you believe we are all capable of change and growth? Do you commit to being better? Do you put in the extra time commitment needed to redevelop your curriculum and provide meaningful feedback for students? Do you forgive yourself when you cannot give more?

Your How

What are your guiding values and principals worded as descriptive action statements for designing curriculum oriented toward social justice? What does authenticity in your classroom look like? What values will directly guide your interactions with students in the classroom? What values and principles for social justice will keep you positive, grounded, and healthy in a world ravaged by colonization, hierarchies, and domination?

---

[46] See page 181 for a definition of Kinesthetic Empathy.

[47] See page 168 for a very brief reference to Culturally Responsive Teaching.

Accountability
Who will help you address your blind spots and biases in this process and hold you accountable to others? How will you center marginalized voices?
Reading
If you have not already, when do you plan to read hooks, Love, Brown, and other inspiring and impactful works by prolific women of color leading us all into the future? If you read hooks, Love, and Brown and others' work and don't feel anything emotionally or physically, are you prepared to reread them to work toward understanding?

Step 2: Design Deep Understandings and Essential Questions for Your Curriculum
Relevance
How will we distinguish merely interesting learning from learning relevant and necessary for social justice? How will you know your teaching is in the important interest of your students?
Essential Questions
Given your beliefs, your intentions, and your *why*, what kind of essential questions are most important for your students to address? Are your essential questions open-ended, thought provoking, able to be revisited again and again, relevant, and do they lead toward dismantling cages and/or building nests?
Enduring Understandings
Given your beliefs and driving *why*, what are the most important understandings for your students to obtain from your teaching? How will you incorporate embodied feeling, believing, thinking, and action for social justice into your enduring understandings?

Goals
What does it look like to meet your classes end goals and how does this align with your students' goals, your own personal goals, and social justice?
Accountability
Who will help you address your blind spots and biases in this process and hold you accountable to others? How will you center marginalized voices? Whose voice is missing from this process?

Step 3: Design Assessments that Both Reach the Depth of Grade-Level Rigor While Addressing Our Deep Understandings for Social Justice
Grade-Level Rigor
What are the key grade-level standards you want to cover in a given unit?
Questions / Tasks
What deep, real-world transferable assessment questions and performance tasks can you design that align to both your deep understandings for social justice and your grade-level standards?
Pedagogies
What assessments aligned to pedagogies oriented toward social justice might you draw from?
Big Assessments
What big assessments align with your desired deep understanding(s) for social justice and transfer of grade-level standards?
Small Assessments
What small assessments can act as a scrapbook leading up to your big assessments?

Understanding for Social Justice
How will you incorporate embodied feeling, believing, thinking, and action for social justice into your big and small assessments?
Rubrics
How will we focus attention on the most important aspects of our assessments and provide a way to measure growth along with streamlined feedback for students?
Nests and Cages
How can your assessments cover both crushing cages and building nests?
Critical Pedagogy
Can you incorporate critical questioning, such as Whose voice is heard? Whose voice is missing? Why are certain voices silenced in the text? How does this relate to your experience? How does this relate to your beliefs? How does this make you feel?
Accountability
Who will help you address your blind spots and biases in this process and hold you accountable to others? How will you center marginalized voices? Whose voice is missing from this process?

Step 4: Create Your Curriculum Scope and Sequence
Pedagogies
How can you draw from multiple pedagogies within the scope of an entire unit?
Alignment Sequence
Where can you place your small assessments leading up to your big assessments within your scope and sequence? Where can

you ensure time for meaningful practice opportunities and feedback?
Alignment to Wholeness
What can you incorporate in your curriculum to reinforce wholeness and finding personal center?
Alignment to Vision, Values, and Principles
How do the daily objectives in your scope and sequence align with your personal values and principals? Or to crushing cages and building nests?
Accountability
Who will help you address your blind spots and biases in this process and hold you accountable to others? Whose voice is missing from this process? How will you center marginalized voices?

Step 5: Design Lesson Plans
Pedagogies
What lesson plan structures can you create that align with pedagogies oriented toward social justice? What lesson plan structures exemplify your values and principals. For example: How will your lesson plans move beyond binaries and borders or make students matter or build community?
Nests and Cages
How will your lesson plans support students in building their interconnected nests? How will your lesson plans work to deconstruct the wires that form oppressive cages?
Rigor
How will you know you are engaging students in rigorous study throughout a lesson? Do your content and questions in the lesson align with grade-level standards? Do your tasks in the

lesson provide meaningful practice opportunities for students? Is the content in your lessons relevant to students?
Alignment to Assessments
Does each lesson lead toward a small and/or big assessment?
Accountability
Who will help you address your blind spots and biases in this process and hold you accountable to others? How will you center marginalized voices? Whose voice is missing from this process?

Step 6: Reflect, Restore, and Repair
Reflect
How will you reflect on your process and adapt as necessary? How do you think your purpose, vision, and beliefs affect the outcomes, the impact, from your curriculum and teaching?
Restore
How will you ground yourself in the pleasure and joy and hope of writing curriculum oriented toward social justice?
Repair
How will you recognize when you cause harm and work to repair said harm? How will you reduce your defensiveness when confronted about your biases and blind spots? How will you create a space where those who have been harmed by you feel empowered to let you know? How will you model both victim and perpetrator in restorative justice?
Accountability
How can you hold yourself accountable to students' learning? Who will help you address your blind spots and biases in this process and hold you accountable to others? How will you

> center marginalized voices? Whose voice is missing from this process?

> **Step ↺: Iterate**
>
> Imagine step "↺" as a spiraling arrow that you overlay over this linear process, to demonstrate that this is not actually a linear step-by-step process but a spiraling process where you take one step forward and potentially two or three steps in a circular motion back around to the beginning again…and again. And that is okay. That is transformative growth.

Alignment

At the end (which really does not exist), *Justice by Design* asks that our lesson plans align with our small assessments, which align with our big assessments. All of this aligns with our grade-level standards and deep enduring understandings for social justice, using pedagogies oriented toward social justice, reaching toward Peggy McIntosh's Phase 5 and wholeness or Glenn Singleton's center or building Jondou Chen's nests and crushing Marilyn Frye's cages. Or put another way:

Using the tenants of backward planning to intentionally create rigorous interdisciplinary curriculum oriented toward social justice and to repair harm that may be caused along the way.

As stated several times earlier: this book was designed for a purpose with guiding intentions. May our collective impact be hopeful, with minimal harm.

Recap and Moving Forward

Putting it all together means:

1. Do your self-work.
2. Design deep understandings oriented toward social justice.
3. Design assessments using pedagogies oriented toward social justice while intertwining grade-level rigor.
4. Design scope and sequence for units incorporating pedagogies oriented toward social justice that lead to your assessments.
5. Design daily lesson plans to incorporate pedagogies oriented toward social justice aligned to your assessments.
6. Reflect, restore, and repair.
↺ Iterate.

The final two steps are especially important, given Emily Style's words that half of our curriculum walks in the room when our students do. We must continually adapt as educators to meet the changing landscapes encompassing our classrooms and worlds.

Chapter 15

Reflect and Restore

Hug Your Failures

— RAUL MATEO MAGDALENO (2019), IDENTIFIES AS
A HISPANIC MOTIVATIONAL SPEAKER WHO
OVERCAME EXTREME ADVERSITY

Guiding Question: How will you thrive as an educator in our current context?

Narrative: Hugging My Failures

"The only way for evil to succeed is for good people to do nothing," These words were ingrained in me growing up. Every school assembly in my high school we repeated them. Every class of students at the private high school I attended on the Upper West Side of Manhattan in New York City had a mantra. "The only way for evil to succeed is for good people to do nothing," was the mantra for the graduating class of 2003 at Trevor Day School. My class.

I loved my high school. I think it set me on a path toward working for educational justice, despite the fact that private schools in New York City represent the epitome of a two-track system. The education I received there was unparalleled in many ways to all of the public institutions I have worked for or observed since. But as with any institution, my high school also lacked in many areas: like socioeconomic and racial diversity, and the education one gets from working with individuals who represent the majority in America, not the 1 percent.

Nonetheless, I consider myself fortunate to have attended; fortunate because my family could afford the huge financial cost to attend; fortunate because my family could also afford to send me to a tutor specializing in supporting adolescent boys with learning disabilities to be able to make it academically at rigorous private high schools; fortunate because of the bonds I developed with my teachers and peers there; fortunate because of the path my high school put me on in life; fortunate because my past educational failures did not dictate my future successes.

Prior to attending Trevor Day School, I attended another more traditional and prestigious private elementary and middle school on the Upper West Side a few blocks away. My elementary and middle school was not a warm and inviting atmosphere for a person with learning disabilities and ADHD. From a young age, I was constantly put down in my class by teachers for not living up to expectations, and I was constantly put down in the playground by my peers for being the overweight kid who failed every class. My elementary and middle school was a place of hierarchy, where only the students with the "right" kind of knowledge mattered, the "right" kind of skills succeeded, or the "right" kind of aspirations of Ivy League colleges prevailed.

From a young age, I found myself failing every assignment and frequently sitting in the principal's office for fighting. Eventually, I ended up severely hurting another child while fighting in school, another child who was overweight and picked on like I was. After the fight, I was asked to leave the school.

I had been kicked out. I had failed at school, and I was only in the 6th grade.

To this day, I hug this failure with all my being. Being kicked out opened the door to the opportunity to attend Trevor Day School from where I would eventually graduate. It was the best opportunity a White boy from the Upper West Side with learning disabilities could hope for after being kicked out of his middle school. It was more than luck to be able to attend another private school in New York—one that was willing to accept a student who had been kicked out of his previous school. I was fortunate. I was privileged. And I know that being kicked out of my middle school was one of the best things to happen to me in life.

As with all of my stories, this one is clearly filled with many intersecting unearned advantages that should often be universal—unearned advantages that helped me to turn my failure into an opportunity for success. But acknowledging the presence of privilege does not diminish the joy I feel in hugging this failure.

Attending my high school set me on a path to where I am now, a life where I still experience failures, and I still work to hug them.

In the two years I spent writing this book, I experienced many failures: failures within my control over, failures outside of my control, failures in which I caused harm, and failures that led to deep personal grief.

On the path toward writing this book, my wife experienced a miscarriage, leading to some of the toughest months of our marriage, including fighting, a lack of compassion, pain, and sadness. In my grief and of the failure to acknowledge the grief in my body, there were many moments when I failed to be the supportive partner my wife needed.

I was part of a team that worked together to found a high school in Minneapolis. For four years, the team felt like family, until things changed. There was constant arguing, blaming, and general toxicity that seemed to shatter our unity and bonds. I failed every time I fueled this toxicity. I failed every time I deflected blame and assumed the worst of my peers. I failed every time I disconnected from my peers and my personal responsibility.

Simultaneously, I found my work role marginalized, and I felt pushed out. Looking back, I failed to deliver for students the way I wanted to. While I deviated more than in previous roles, I failed to deviate as much as I would have liked from replicating the status quo.

For me, hugging failures is about finding opportunities, finding hope, finding ways to repair, finding center, finding wholeness, finding acceptance, and finding peace.

Six months after my wife's miscarriage, we were blessed to get pregnant again (I say "we," though I realize my wife carried the vast majority of the burden and pain), and now we have the most healthy and beautiful and amazing baby girl. Our marriage is stronger having worked through the pain and made it. Parenting seems easier, having strengthened our relationship and lessened our anxiety, knowing we can make it through the toughest nights.

As for the breaking up of a work family, as sad and painful as it was, led me to accept the offer of a new job when I was approached. It was an offer I never would have pursued or accepted had I still felt like part of my founding work family. It has turned out to be the job and the place I needed to be as a father of a three-year-old and newborn, a job where I can still impact educators and students but have a much more flexible work schedule.

While there was pain and harm I inflicted and felt in each of my past failures, there was always opportunity. In some instances, the opportunity was finding a new path. In some instances, the opportunity was personal growth, practicing humility, and asking others how I can repair the hurt I caused. In some instances, the opportunity was to forgive, both others and myself. Finding the opportunity makes it easier to accept my failures, easier to hug my failures.

I need to accept all the failure to take an honest look at myself in the mirror, to begin to understand my truths. I cannot understand my students or my content until I understand myself, and I need to understand both my students and my content to teach it.

I also find it difficult to love my students until I love myself. From self-love I find the strength to honestly look in the mirror and understand that I matter, and my students matter. From self-love I find the power to repair harm that I have caused without getting defensive, and I find the power to repair with and love those who have inflicted harm upon me.

Justice is love.

Self-Reflection

Self-reflection is a cornerstone of learning whether referring to students' transferring skills and knowledge to grow as agents of change or teachers developing their practice to grow as agents of change.

After conducting the largest meta-analysis of meta-analyses done on effective practices in education, Jon Hattie (2019), who self-identifies as a Kiwi pakeha, Australian, retired laureate professor, director of The Hattie Family Foundation, husband, father, and grandfather, claims in *Visible Learning for Teachers* that, "The major argument... underlying powerful impacts in our schools relates to how we think! It is a set of mind frames that underpin our every action and decision in a school; it is a belief that we are evaluators, change agents, adaptive learning experts, seekers of feedback about our impact, engaged in dialogue and challenge, and developers of trust with all, and that we see opportunity in error, and are keen to spread the message about the power, fun, and impact that we have on learning." I would argue that when Hattie says, "how we think," he is referring to more than intellectualizing; he is also referring to beliefs, to embodied understandings, to feelings and to what we do with this.

To continually develop our mindsets, our beliefs, or feelings as educators, we need to reflect. To understand our impact, we need to reflect, evaluate where we have been, and listen. To adapt to our shared futures, we need to reflect on and understand our past. To give meaningful feedback, we must demonstrate accepting it. To cultivate trust, we must trust our students and understand our students, which requires us to understand ourselves and our world; we must be vulnerable, and we must acknowledge and work to repair harm when we cause it; and we must even trust ourselves.

Deep self-reflection requires vulnerability; it requires that we acknowledge the beautiful and the ugly. Deep self-reflection requires self-love. To restate Sharon Salzberg's (2017) sentiments, real self-love comes with a powerful recognition that we are already whole, despite our areas for growth. "It is a state where we allow ourselves to be seen clearly by ourselves and by others, and in turn, we offer clear seeing to the world around us. It is a love that heals." Deep self-reflection requires seeing clearly. Deep self-reflection is a step toward repairing and restoring.

Note that here we come back to love; or maybe we never left. Love allows all members in our classrooms to engage, learn, and grow, including ourselves.

Love is power. Love is justice. God is love. And real love starts when you look in the mirror.

You deserve all the love in the world.

You do not have to earn love.

You simply have to exist.

(Salzberg, 2017)

Yes, and…

Your students deserve all the love in the world.

Your students do not have to earn love.

Your students simply have to exist.

Believe in love.

Justice by Design is love by design.

Recap and Moving Forward

This book both opens and ends with self-reflection. Self-reflection is important to doing the work with discernment. It is a key to intentionality. However, just reading is not doing the work or even self-reflecting. The work comes from personalizing the reading; understanding and shifting your embodied beliefs; recognizing, invoking, and harnessing your embodied feelings; and ultimately writing and teaching curriculum oriented toward social justice.

We have not arrived as a nation. We have not arrived as an educational system. I have not personally arrived as a cisgender White man. But I am working on it. I am working toward social justice and personal healing, toward wholeness[48] and center[49], toward abolitionist teaching[50], pleasure activism[51], real love[52], and *Justice by Design*. Let's work together.

---

[48] A reference to Peggy McIntosh, *Phase Theory*
[49] A reference to Glenn Singleton, *Courageous Conversations*
[50] A reference to Bettina L. Love, *We Want to Do More Than Survive*.
[51] A reference to Adrienne Maree Brown, *Emergent Strategy* and *Pleasure Activism*.
[52] A reference to Sharon Salzberg, *Real Love*.

Gratitude

To my daughters, my partner, my sister, my parents, and aunts for your constant support throughout this process and before that too.

To my Accountability Panel including, Alex Harp, E.V.B., Joe Beaulieu, and Joetta Wright, for your loving accountability, teachings, and encouragement.

References

Adams, M., Bell, L. A., & Griffin, P. (1997). Teaching for diversity and social justice: A sourcebook. New York, NY: Routledge.

Agarwal-Rangnath, R., Dover, A. G., & Henning, N. (2016). *Preparing to teach social studies for social justice: Becoming a renegade.* New York, NY: Teachers College Press.

Barker, M., Iantaffi, A., & Lester, C. N. (2019). *Life isn't binary: On being both, beyond, and in-between.* London, England: Jessica Kingsley.

Battalora, J. M. (2013) *Birth of a white nation: the invention of white people and its relevance today* Houston, Tex: Strategic Book Publishing,

Battiste, M. A. (2017). *Decolonizing education: Nourishing the learning spirit.*

Bell, L. A., Roberts, R. A., Kayhan Irani, and Brett Murphy (2008): The Storytelling Project Curriculum: Learning About Race and Racism through Storytelling and the Arts

Bellisario, K. & Donovan, L. (2012). Voices from the field: Teachers' views on the relevance of arts integration. Cambridge, MA: Lesley University. (https://www.artsedsearch.org/study/voices-from-the-field-teachers-views-on-the-relevance-of-arts-integration/)

Brenchley, P. (2011). *In America, education is still the great equalizer.* Retrieved August, 2020, from https://blog.ed.gov/2011/12/in-america-education-is-still-the-great-equalizer/

Brown, A. M. (2017). *Emergent strategy: shaping change, changing worlds.* Chico, CA: AK Press.

Brown, A. M. (2019). *Pleasure activism: The politics of feeling good.* Edinburgh, United Kingdom: AK Press.

Brown, A. M. (2020). *We will not cancel us: And other dreams of transformative justice.* Chico, CA: AK Press.

Bush, G. W. (2006). Transcript of Bush's address to N.A.A.C.P. Retrieved August, 2020, from https://www.nytimes.com/2006/07/20/washington/20text-bush.html

Cahalan, M., Perna, L. W., Yamashita, M., Wright, J. & Santillan, S (2018). *Indicators of Higher Education Equity in the United States — 2018 Historical Trend Report.* Washington, DC: The Pell Institute for the Study of Opportunity in Higher Education,

REFERENCES

Council for Opportunity in Education (COE), and Alliance for Higher Education and Democracy of the University of Pennsylvania (PennAHEAD)

Chen, J.C. (2018). *On Nests and Cages: Facilitating Toward Just Possibilities*, https://nationalseedproject.org/itemid-fix/blogger/jondouchen

Chen, J. D. (2013). Where Do I Even Begin? Understanding Myself and My SEED Work Using Phase Theory. Retrieved August, 2020, from https://nationalseedproject.org/Leader-Essays/where-do-i-even-begin-understanding-myself-and-my-seed-work-using-phase-theory

Coffey, H. (2015). Critical literacy. K–12 teaching and learning from the UNC School of Education. Retrieved August, 2020, from www.learnnc.org/lp/pages/4437

Conway, E., & Batalden, P. (2015). *Like magic? ("Every system is perfectly designed...")*. Retrieved August, 2020, from http://www.ihi.org/communities/blogs/origin-of-every-system-is-perfectly-designed-quote

Crenshaw, K. (2015, September) *Why intersectionality can't wait*. Washington Post.

Daggett, W. (2009). Rigor and relevance: Preparing students for a 21st century world. *Seen*. Southeast Education Network. Available: https://www.seenmagazine.us/Articles/Article-Detail/ArticleId/207/Rigor-and-Relevance

Delpit, L. (2012). "Multiplication is for white people": raising expectations for other people's children. New York: New Press: Distributed by Perseus Distribution.

Economy Policy Institute (EPI, 2017): *EPI analysis of Current Population Survey Outgoing Rotation Group microdata*. go.epi.org/genderpaygap

Einstein, A. (1952). Education for independent thought. *New York Times*, 5.

Emdin, C. (2017). *For White Folks Who Teach in the Hood ... and the Rest of Y'all Too Reality Pedagogy and Urban Education*. Beacon Pr.

Erkens, C., & Schimmer, T. (2017). *Essential Assessment: Six Tenets for Bringing Hope, Efficacy, and Achievement to the Classroom Deepen Teachers Understanding of Assessment to Meet Standards and Generate a Culture of Learning*. Solution Tree.

ERN. (2016, April 06). RELEASE: Americans Spending At Least $1.5 Billion in College Remediation Courses; Middle Class Pays the Most. Retrieved August, 2020, from https://edreformnow.org/accountability/release-americans-spending-at-least-1-5-billion-in-college-remediation-courses-middle-class-pays-the-most/

Fact Sheet: Focusing Higher Education on Student Success. (2015, July 27). Retrieved August, 2020, from https://www.ed.gov/news/press-releases/fact-sheet-focusing-higher-education-student-success

Feldman, J. (2019). *Grading for equity: What it is, why it matters, and how it can transform schools and classrooms*. Thousand Oaks, California: Corwin.

Freire, P. (1985). *The politics of education: Culture, power, and liberation*. South Hadley, Mass: Bergin & Garvey.

Freire, P. (1997). *Pedagogy of the heart*. New York: Continuum.

Freire, P. (2018). *Pedagogy of the oppressed*. Bloomsbury, Academics.

Frye, M. (1983). The Politics of Reality: Essays in Feminist Theory. Trumansburg, NY: The Crossing Press.

Gazibara, S. (2020). "Head, Heart and Hands Learning" - A challenge for contemporary education. *Journal of Education Culture and Society, 4*(1), 71-82.

Generative Somatics. (2006). What is a Politicized Somatics? Retrieved August, 2020, 2020, from https://generativesomatics.org/wp-content/uploads/2019/10/Copy-of-What-is-a-politicized-somatics.pdf

Grey, M. C. (2001). *The outrageous pursuit of hope: Prophetic dreams for the twenty-first century*. New York, NY: Crossroad Pub.

Harp A. Correspondent, editing message to author, August, 2020

Hattie, J. (2019). *Visible learning for teachers: Maximizing impact on learning*. London: Routledge.

Hindery, R. K. (2018). *OPRF in spotlight as NPR live broadcast explores education, race and 'America to Me'*. Pioneer Press, October 30, 2018, 2:25 p.m.

hooks, b. (2000a). *Feminism is for everybody: Passionate politics*. Cambridge, MA: South End Press.

hooks, b. (2000b). *Building a Community of Love: Shambhala Sun, 1st January, 2000,* https://plumvillage.org/about/thich-nhat-hanh/interviews-with-thich-nhat-hanh/interview-with-bell-hooks-january-1-2000/

hooks, b. (2003). *Teaching community: A pedagogy of hope*. New York: Routledge.

Jefferson, T. (1814). *Thomas Jefferson to Peter Carr, 7 September 1814*, Founders Online, National Archives, https://founders.archives.gov/documents/Jefferson/03-07-02-0462. [Original source: The Papers of Thomas Jefferson,

Retirement Series, vol. 7, 28 November 1813 to 30 September 1814, ed. J. Jefferson Looney. Princeton: Princeton University Press, 2010, pp. 636–642.]

Johnson, D. W., Johnson, R. T., & Holubec, E. J. (2008). *Cooperation in the classroom*. Edina, MN: Interaction Book.

Johnson, D. W., & Johnson, R. T. (2002). *Multicultural education and human relations: Valuing diversity*. Upper Saddle River, NJ: Prentice Hall.

Johnson, R. (2018). *Embodied social justice*. Abingdon, Oxon: Routledge, an imprint of the Taylor & Francis Group.

Kendi, I. X. (2016). *Stamped from the beginning: The definitive history of racist ideas in America*. New York: Nation Books.

King, M.L. (1967), *last presidential address to the Southern Christian Leadership Conference on August 16, 1967*.

Kreber, C., Klampfleitner, M., McCune, V., Bayne, S., & Knottenbelt, M. (2007). *What do you mean by "authentic"? A comparative review of the literature on conceptions of authenticity in teaching*. Adult Education Quarterly, 58(1), 22–43.

Ladson-Billings, G. (1994). *The dreamkeepers*. San Francisco: Jossey-Bass Publishing Co.

Ladson-Billings, G. (2014) *Culturally Relevant Pedagogy 2.0: a.k.a. the Remix*. Harvard Educational Review: April 2014, Vol. 84, No. 1, pp. 74-84.

Lamott, A. (2019). *Bird by bird: Some instructions on writing and life*. New York: Anchor Books.

Lewis, N., & Lockwood, B. (2019, December 17). The Hidden Cost of Incarceration. Retrieved August, 2020, from https://www.themarshallproject.org/2019/12/17/the-hidden-cost-of-incarceration

Lexico. (2020). Social Justice. Lexico.com dictionary. https://www.lexico.com/en/definition/social_justice

Living Justice Press (n.d.) The Indigenous Origins of Circles and How Non-Natives Learned About Them. Retrieved August, 2020, from http://www.livingjusticepress.org/?SEC=0F6FA816-E094-4B96-8F39-9922F67306E5: Living Justice Press

Love, B. L. (2019). *We want to do more than survive: Abolitionist teaching and the pursuit of educational freedom*.

Magdaleno, R. M. 2020 National Summit for Courageous Conversation, New Orleans, LA, October 2020.

Mann, H. (1848). *Twelfth Annual Report of the Board of Education, together with the Twelfth Annual Report of the Secretary of the Board*.

Retrieved August, 2020, from https://archives.lib.state.ma.us/handle/2452/204731

McIntosh, P. (1983). Interactive phases of curricular re-vision: A feminist perspective. *Center for Research on Women*, 1-36.

McIntosh, P. (1981, October). The Study of Women in the Liberal Arts Curriculum. In *Forum for Liberal Education* (Vol. 4, No. 1, p. n1).

McKenzie, M. (2016). *Solidarity Struggle: How People of Color Succeed and Fail at Showing up for Each Other in the Fight for Freedom.* Black Girl Dangerous Press.

McTighe, J., & Wiggins, G. P. (2013). *Essential questions: Opening doors to student understanding.* Alexandria, VA: ASCD.

Menakem, R. (2017). *My grandmother's hands: Racialized trauma and the pathway to mending our hearts and bodies.* Las Vegas, NV: Central Recovery Press.

National Summit Courageous Conversations (2019).

No Child Left Behind Act of 2001, P.L. 107-110, 20 U.S.C.

Office of Superintendent of Public Instruction (OSPI) (2011); Bias and Sensitivity Review of the Common Core State Standards in English Language Arts and Mathematics, State Report.

Palmer, P. J. (1998). The courage to teach: exploring the inner landscape of a teacher's life. San Francisco, CA: Jossey-Bass.

Palmer, P. J. (1993). *To know as we are known: Education as a spiritual journey.* San Francisco: Harper San Francisco.

Papola, A. (2013). *Critical literacy, common core, and close reading*. Colorado Reading Journal, 46–50.

Agarwal-Rangnath, Ruchi. Preparing to Teach Social Studies for Social Justice (Becoming a Renegade) (p. 130). Teachers College Press. Kindle Edition.

Peter, J. (2017). *The new human rights movement: Reinventing the economy to end oppression.*

Quoteresearch. (2014, April 6). They may forget what you said, but they will never forget how you made them feel. Retrieved August, 2020, from https://quoteinvestigator.com/2014/04/06/they-feel/

Reardon, S.F. (2013), *The Widening Income Achievement Gap.* Educational Leadership May 2013 | Volume 70 | Number 8 Faces of Poverty Pages 10-16.

Rhodes, J. A., & Milby, T. M. (2016). *Advancing teacher education and curriculum development through study abroad programs.* Hershey, PA: Information Science Reference.

Ripper, V. (Director). (2012). *Occupy Love.* Independent.

Ritchhart, R. (2015). *Creating cultures of thinking: The 8 forces we must master to truly transform our schools.*

Rosenthal, R, and L. Jacobsen (1968). Pygmalion in the classroom: teacher expectation and pupils' intellectual development. New York: Holt, Rinehart and Winston.

Ruiz, M. (1997). *The four agreements: a practical guide to personal freedom.* San Rafael, CA: Amber-Allen Pub.

Salzberg, S. (2017). *Real love: the art of mindful connection.* First edition. New York: Flatiron Books.

Schwegler, A. F. (2019). Academic Rigor: A Comprehensive Definition.

The Sentencing Project (2016). *The Color of Justice: Racial and Ethnic Disparities in State Prisons.* https://www.sentencingproject.org/publications/color-of-justice-racial-and-ethnic-disparity-in-state-prisons/

Seuss. (1990). *Oh, the places you'll go!* Random House.

Sinek, S. (2009). *Start with why: how great leaders inspire everyone to take action.* New York: Portfolio.

Singleton, G. E. (2015). *Courageous conversations about race: A field guide for achieving equity in schools.* Thousand Oaks, CA: Corwin, A SAGE Company.

Singleton, J. (2015). HEAD, HEART AND HANDS MODEL FOR TRANSFORMATIVE LEARNING: PLACE AS CONTEXT FOR CHANGING SUSTAINABILITY VALUES. *Journal of Sustainability Education, 9,* 2151-7452.

Sium, A. & Ritskes, E. (2013). *Speaking truth to power: indigenous storytelling as an act of living resistance.* Decolonization: Indigeneity, Education & Society, 2, I- X.

Style, E (1988), *Curriculum As Window and Mirror.* Listening for All Voices, Oak Knoll School monograph, Summit, NJ.

Sue, D. W. (2010). *Microaggressions: More than just race.* Psychology Today, 17.

TNTP (2018). *The opportunity myth.* New York, NY: Author. Retrieved September 29, 2018, from https://tntp.org/assets/documents/TNTP_The-Opportunity-Myth_Web.pdf

U.S. Bureau of Labor Statistics (2020) *Learn more, earn more: Education leads to higher wages, lower unemployment,* Career Outlook, U.S. Bureau of Labor Statistics, May 2020.

Vagle, N. D., & Reeves, D. (2015). *Design in 5: Essential phases to create engaging assessment practice.* Bloomington, IN: Solution Tree Press.

Van Der Valk, A. (2014). Peggy McIntosh: Beyond the Knapsack. Retrieved August, 2020, from https://www.tolerance.org/magazine/spring-2014/peggy-mcintosh-beyond-the-knapsack?elq=a68db9104bc24fedb66c1473d9d3d30d

VanDeCarr, P. (2015) Storytelling and Social Change: A guide for activists, organizations and social entrepreneurs.

Vanden Branden, E. Correspondent, editing message to author, August, 2020

Villanueva, E. (2018). *Decolonizing wealth: Indigenous wisdom to heal divides and restore balance.*

Visible Learning. (2020). Retrieved August, 2020, from https://visible-learning.org/

Warren, M. R. (2010). *Fire in the Heart: How White Activists Embrace Racial Justice.* Oxford, NY: Oxford University Press.

Waziyatawin & Yellow, B. M. (2005). *For indigenous eyes only: A decolonization handbook.* Santa Fe: School of American Research.

Webb, R. Correspondent, in-person conversation with author, October, 2019

Wiggins, G. P., & McTighe, J. (2008). *Understanding by design.* Alexandria, VA: Association for Supervision and Curriculum Development.

Wiggins, G. P., & McTighe, J. (2012). *The understanding by design guide to advanced concepts in creating and reviewing units.* Heinle ELT.

Winters, A. (n.d.). *Using Talking Circles in the classroom.* Retrieved August, 2020 from https://www.heartland.edu/documents/idc/talkingCircleClassroom.pdf

Wolff, EN (2017). *Household Wealth Trends in the United States, 1962 to 2016: Has Middle Class Wealth Recovered?* Working Paper No. 24085 November 2017 JEL No. D31,J15.

Wun, C (2014) The Anti-Black Order of No Child Left Behind: Using Lacanian psychoanalysis and critical race theory to examine NCLB, Educational Philosophy and Theory, 46:5, 462-474.

Zehr, H. (2014). *The little book of restorative justice.* Good Books, New York, NY

About the Author

Ian McLaughlin was born and raised in NYC. He grew up in the private school system there with learning disabilities, namely Dyslexia and ADHD. With a desire to support other individuals with (dis)abilities, he started his path in education first as a Special Education teacher, then school administrator, and is now teacher educator in Minnesota. He also founded justicebydesign.org in 2018 which provides curricular materials oriented toward social justice for educators. His curriculum is currently in use in high school and college classrooms across the U.S.

Throughout Ian's journey, his intention of supporting scholars with (dis)abilities naturally led him to work on better understanding intersecting systems of oppression including ableism, White supremacy and racism, classism, sexism, heteronormativity, ageism, nativism, and more. As a White man, he has found it his responsibility to support dismantling oppressive systems that he has personally benefited from; while simultaneously following the lead of those who have been most marginalized into the future.

www.ingramcontent.com/pod-product-compliance
Lightning Source LLC
Chambersburg PA
CBHW072146100526
44589CB00015B/2113